JOB SEARCH NAVIGATOR

LINDA A. HENDERSON
MARTHA D. ADAMSON

Prentice Hall

Upper Saddle River, New Jersey 07458

Library of Congress Cataloging-in-Publication Data

Henderson, Linda A.
     Job search navigator / Linda A. Henderson , Martha D. Adamson.
        p.   cm.
     Includes index.
     ISBN 0-13-917907-0
     1. Job hunting.   I. Adamson, Martha D.   II. Title.
HF5382.7.H46   1998
650.14—dc21   98-17799
                                                                                    CIP

Publisher: *Carol Carter*
Acquisitions Editor: *Sue Bierman*
Managing Editor: *Mary Carnis*
Production: *Holcomb Hathaway, Inc.*
Production Liaison: *Glenn Johnston*
Director of Manufacturing and Production: *Bruce Johnson*
Manufacturing Buyer: *Marc Bove*
Cover Design: *Marianne Frasco*
Cover Art: *Stephanie Henderson*
Editorial Assistant: *Amy Diehl*
Marketing Manager: *Jeff McIlroy*
Marketing Assistant: *Christopher Eastman*

 © 1999 by Prentice-Hall, Inc.
Simon & Schuster / A Viacom Company
Upper Saddle River, New Jersey 07458

Printed in the United States of America

10 9 8 7 6 5 4 3 2 1

ISBN 0-13-917907-0

Prentice-Hall International (UK) Limited, *London*
Prentice-Hall of Australia Pty. Limited, *Sydney*
Prentice-Hall Canada Inc., *Toronto*
Prentice-Hall Hispanoamericana, S.A., *Mexico*
Prentice-Hall of India Private Limited, *New Delhi*
Prentice-Hall of Japan, Inc., *Tokyo*
Simon & Schuster Asia Pte. Ltd., *Singapore*
Editora Prentice-Hall do Brasil, Ltda., *Rio de Janeiro*

CONTENTS

4 Writing Your Resume   57

SECTION TWO—CHARTING YOUR COURSE   93

5 Job Market Information   95

6 Networking   111

7 Your Correspondence   125

Section Three—Sailing Away   139

8 Job Search Management   141

9 Applications and References   151

10 All About Interviews   159

11 Stay the Course: The Key to Landing Opportunities   167

DEDICATIONS

To my husband, Dan Fields, who has been a wonderful personal and professional friend. To my family who have always been proud of my accomplishments and to my many wonderful friends who have offered support and encouragement throughout all of my career endeavors. To my nephew, Dylan, who brings joy and inspiration to my life; may he benefit from this book as he progresses in his life's journey. To my many fine teachers and mentors who, over the years, have guided me. And, most of all, to Martha, who has been delightful to work with throughout our own journey of writing this book.

Linda A. Henderson

For my parents, who taught me to find my way past the obstacles that litter our lives, for my husband, who has demonstrated lifelong creativity, flexibility, and positive perseverance in his own career, to my friend Linda, who pushed and prodded me to believe in the reality of this project, and to my children who are embarking on their own careers—may they find this information helpful.

Martha D. Adamson

PREFACE

Job Search Navigator is designed as a navigational guide to your career and job search journey. The most appropriate job search is not when you simply find a job, but when you find a job that's *right* for you. It is important to find a job that you love, at a salary you find satisfying, in a location you prefer. To achieve this goal, *Job Search Navigator* guides you through three important job search phases: "Preparing for Your Voyage," "Charting Your Course," and "Sailing Away." *Job Search Navigator* has been carefully designed to take you through each step of a comprehensive job search. Each worksheet prepares you for the necessary job search steps. When you are properly prepared, you not only feel more confident in your job search, but you are more knowledgeable about the possibilities. If your search is done well, you will also see how your job fits into your overall career and life management plan, and how it fulfills and draws on your values, needs, interests, skills, knowledge, and abilities.

This book is based on the personal and professional experiences of the authors, who have each worked with thousands of job seekers from different backgrounds and professions throughout North America. We have learned from each job seeker and want to share that information with you.

The worksheets will prove most useful to you if you complete all of the exercises in the order presented. All of the steps are important in helping you sort through the infinite choices you face as you progress through your career.

Have fun with this and learn from it. Good luck in your ventures to come.

ACKNOWLEDGMENTS

We wish to acknowledge the many clients who, over the years, have shared their insights and experiences with us as they progressed on their own job search journeys. We would like to thank Dana Meltzer for encouraging us to submit this manuscript. The Prentice-Hall group has been excellent to work with and we want to thank Todd Rossell and Sue Bierman, our Editors, and Amy Diehl for all of their support throughout this project. Our special thanks to Gay Pauley and the production team, who have been a joy to work with as they turned our word processing efforts into a beautifully laid out, functional work. We want to thank Brenda Rizer and Gordon Henderson for their tireless editing assistance. We are grateful to our cover artist, Stephanie Henderson, who translated our concept into a stunning visual image.

Along the way, many other people have helped us shape and produce this book. We would like to thank our reviewers for their many helpful suggestions and encouragement. These include Gwendolyn Burgess, Alvin Community College; Rita Delude, New Hampshire Community Technical College; Susan Ekberg, Webster University; Pat Schutz, Mesa State College; Monica Zeigler, Pace University; and Gary Kramer, Brigham Young University.

Linda A. Henderson, Ph.D.
Martha D. Adamson, M.A.

The flags you'll see throughout this book have a meaning . . .

In keeping with this book's nautical theme (and for fun!), we've used throughout the book the signal flags flown by naval and other ships to communicate with one another. These flags might be used when radio communication is down, in times of radio silence, or simply to identify a ship or its country of origin and so forth. The flags represent an important maritime language.

On the chapter-opening pages and on the worksheets in this book, you'll see a variety of flags. Each individual flag represents a specific number or letter. For example:

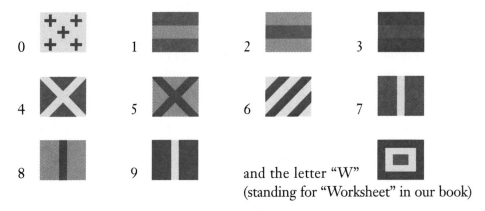

and the letter "W" (standing for "Worksheet" in our book)

You'll see that Chapter 1 has at its start this flag, ▬, corresponding to the number 1. Chapter 2 uses this flag, ▬, and so forth. The worksheets use the "W" flag, ▣, and then two numeral flags; for example, Worksheet 3.4 will use these two flags: ▮ and ✕.

These flags have been used through the decades to help sea-going men and women navigate a sure course on challenging seas. As you navigate your own job search course, we hope they act as a reminder to you that you are not alone on the sea and that it's vital to communicate with others!

INTRODUCTION

YOUR CAREER JOURNEY

Most people wouldn't embark on a long journey to an unfamiliar place without consulting a map, charting a course, planning carefully what to bring and what to do along the way, and even setting goals for daily destinations. Yet every day, thousands of people embark on a job search without any plan or direction. Conducting an effective and thorough job search is one of the most challenging activities that you face. As a graduate entering the full-time work force, or as a seasoned job holder faced with the need or desire to change jobs or career direction, you may find it difficult to know where to start. You may also wish to organize your credentials in preparation for the unexpected or to be ready to make a change if an opportunity presents itself. A job search done poorly may either make your situation worse or not provide the improvement for which you had hoped. A job search done well, with insight into your needs and desires, carefully planned and executed, can result in the job of your dreams and position you for future rewards.

Job Search Navigator has been designed to provide you with the necessary guidance in the job search journey. It has been developed by experienced career development counselors who have had many years of experience in guiding hundreds of people from many kinds of jobs and professions through the job search journey to satisfying destinations.

LIFE MANAGEMENT

A job search, like a journey, should be carefully planned. However, the search should be preceded by a carefully thought-out plan based upon research and the development of a plan for the management of your life. The development of a life management plan involves looking carefully at your goals, values, direction, and the issues that are important to you and your family. These include health and personal habits, family and other important relationships, environment, vocation and avocations, personal growth, leisure and recreation, lifestyle, and financial considerations. This examination and decision-making process provides a larger background against which a consistent job search strategy can be developed.

JOB TARGETING

Job targeting is like choosing your destination. It is the process of carefully identifying the characteristics that you would like to replicate in your new position by looking at the elements that you found to be satisfying in your previous positions. This assessment includes examining your previous jobs and educational experiences, work groups, companies, industries, and geographic locations. Questions that you might ask yourself include: What is my ideal position? What type of company do I want to work for? What traits am

I looking for in a boss or work group? Do I want a large or small company? Public or private? What industry am I interested in? Do I want to work in the city or the suburbs? What components of a job are important to me? Is a challenge important? Hours? Flexibility? Knowing your job target is very important in identifying organizations and opportunities that match it. Later in your job search, job targeting provides criteria against which to evaluate a job offer.

SELF-ASSESSMENT

Before you start your journey, you need to take stock of your background, skills, life and work experiences, accomplishments, education, and training. These elements are important in the preparation of both your resume and upcoming interviews. They change over time as you gain experience in your career, learn new skills, and gain further knowledge. It is important to periodically review and update your portfolio of skills and talents as you move through your career. You should also review your positions, job functions, and accomplishments annually to assess where you have been and decide where you are going. This information becomes the essence of your resume and prepares you for interviews as well as further career planning.

RESUME DEVELOPMENT

A resume is like a passport. If done well, it will get you to the first stop of your destination: the job interview. It is a brief, prioritized, written presentation of your employment or professional history. A well-designed and well-constructed resume acts as a sales tool for you. It is a comprehensive yet brief summary of the experiences, skills, knowledge, and credentials that will support your current job search.

JOB RESEARCH

Like planning for a trip to unfamiliar territory, advance research and planning can make the difference between a memorable, delightful journey and a miserable, unsuccessful one. The heart of a well-targeted job search begins in the library and, increasingly, on the Internet. A wealth of information is available regarding companies, industries, employment trends, and community and corporate leaders. Databases and directories make accessing information easy. Your job search strategy should consist of regular trips to the public library and regular planned excursions into the wealth of information available at Web sites, through listservers, and in computer-accessible databases. From your research, make a list of employers that you are interested in contacting for employment opportunities. Start with a small number of companies, contact them, and then add more to your list as necessary. A small number to start with helps to keep your search manageable and organized.

JOB PROSPECTING

Once you have chosen the amenities and characteristics of your destination, you often find that you have a choice of locations that will please you. The same is true of your job target. There will probably be many choices of employers who have jobs that match your job target. The telephone is the best, most convenient means of conducting your job prospecting efforts. Effective telephone prospecting requires proper preparation, practice, and mental attitude. You need to develop a script that you can use when calling employers to set up appointments. Set goals for yourself and make your calls regularly. It is also an excellent way to meet fellow professionals and uncover job opportunities.

NETWORKING

Oftentimes, the very best way to determine the pros and cons of your selected journey can be through talking with people who have been there, or know something about it. In a job search, this process of obtaining advice, information, and/or referrals is called *networking*. Everyone you meet is a potential networking contact. To network most effectively, you need to clearly communicate your job target and suggest specific ways your contact can be of assistance to you. Professional associations and community groups also provide excellent networking opportunities.

INTERVIEWING

The interview is like going through immigration. If you have followed the rules and prepared properly, you will be admitted; if not, you will be excluded. The interview is the culmination of your planning, research, and preparation. Careful preparation is critical. Review your professional history, focusing on your strengths and accomplishments. Practice answering commonly asked interview questions. Research the organization. Know what questions you would like to ask the interviewer. Show an interest in the job. Follow up immediately after the interview.

JOB SEARCH MANAGEMENT

As you collect the information, tools, and skills you need to start your journey, you will be most successful if you carefully manage your time, information, and goals for your daily and weekly progress. Develop an action plan that includes these components: prospecting and lead development, research, appointment and interview scheduling, follow-up, and record keeping. It is very important to keep well-organized and up-to-date records during your job search.

Knowing how to conduct a job search is not enough. You must have the courage to implement what you have learned, confidence in yourself, and the perseverance needed to work hard at your search. It is essential to maintain a positive attitude and a bright outlook. Your career/life management plan should be followed diligently and persistently as you seek a new and satisfactory position.

Your job search can be an exciting adventure to find fulfilling employment that matches your ideal job target. Along the way, you will meet many interesting people who will become part of your new network. We wish you the best on your career journey. Let *Job Search Navigator* be your guide.

PREPARING
FOR YOUR
VOYAGE

1

LIFE MANAGEMENT

INTRODUCTION

Many people go through their careers as if they're on a guided tour to a random destination. They let circumstances and other people move them through successive jobs without much input from themselves. The result is often a sense of regret at the end of their work lives as they look back and realize that they lost sight of early goals and interests and never accomplished what they had hoped to achieve as young people. Life management is a decision-making process that involves an appraisal of your life's direction and goals. By engaging in the life management process at the start of your career and then on a regular basis thereafter, you will be able to cope better with challenges when faced with a turning point in your life, thereby exerting more influence on the course of your career.

Life management includes examining eight broad areas of your life: Values; Health and Habits; Family, Extended Family and Friends; Career/Vocation/Avocation; Geographic Location; Personal Growth and Development; Leisure and Recreation; and Money Matters. In each area, you will examine what is important to you and which aspects you find satisfying or dissatisfying; then you will develop a wish list for changes and improvements. Finally, using these areas as a foundation, you can create a personal mission statement that you can use to guide your decision making in your life and career.

LIFE PLANNING EXERCISES

Values are the driving force within your life that influence your goals and choices. In daily life, you are continually faced with situations that demand thought, decision, and action. Many of these compete with one another for time, energy, and resources. Knowledge of your values will help you chart a course through life that will be in harmony with your spirit and will make decision making easier.

Values can be defined as qualities that are meaningful to you. They are tendencies for you to prefer one kind of outcome over another. Your system of values provides a motivating force to your behavior. Values are dynamic, changing in importance as you age and go through personal life changes. You need to examine your values periodically to ensure that your life is moving in harmony with your current beliefs. Often, when your career or life is moving in a direction away from your values, you will have a feeling of dissatisfaction or stress. By understanding and resolving that conflict, you will move into harmony. It is also wise to discuss your values with significant people in your life. Recognizing where you have value differences with those who are important in your life can be the basis for resolving interpersonal conflicts.

Values Hierarchy

Read the list of values below. Then go back and rank them in importance to you using this scale:

1 = Always Important   2 = Sometimes Important   3 = Rarely Important

_____ A well-balanced and integrated life

_____ Beauty in nature, arts, and environment

_____ Social affiliation; recognition, respect, and admiration

_____ Inner peace, harmony, and balance

_____ Contribution to society; leaving a legacy

_____ Family security

_____ Equality, impartiality, and lack of prejudice

_____ Intellectual challenge

_____ Using judgment, wisdom, and decision-making skills

_____ Mature love and intimacy

_____ Personal freedom, independence, flexibility, and free choice

_____ Physical activity

_____ Pleasure, enjoyment, and leisure

_____ Prosperity and a comfortable lifestyle

_____ Salvation

_____ Self-esteem, self-respect, and a feeling of self-worth

_____ Exciting, stimulating work and life

_____ Working on the frontiers of knowledge

_____ Power and authority

_____ Competition against others

_____ Advancement, growth, and seniority

_____ Creativity in ideas, procedures, or projects

Now, go back and select six of your "Always Important" values that must be present in your next job; write them below. See the next page for examples.

_____   _____

_____   _____

_____   _____

EXAMPLE 1

Lakesha is a recent graduate with a degree in biochemistry. She found that her top six values were:

- a well-balanced and integrated life
- contribution to society; leaving a legacy
- using judgment, wisdom, and decision-making skills
- exciting, stimulating work and life
- working on the frontiers of knowledge
- creativity in ideas, procedures, or projects

Based on this information, Lakesha decided to look for a job with a large research and development organization working on developing pharmaceutical products. She felt that this kind of organization would give her a chance to work on cutting-edge research and have many opportunities for growth.

EXAMPLE 2

Charles was unhappy with his retail management position. When his job was eliminated due to downsizing, he examined his values and discovered that his top six were:

- social affiliation
- family security
- prosperity and a comfortable lifestyle
- power and authority
- competition against others
- creativity

This information helped him decide to focus on his sales skills in finding a new job, rather than his management skills. He wanted to try to rely on his own efforts rather than those of a staff to achieve his personal and business goals.

Health and Habits

Your ability to pursue your goals fully can be positively or negatively affected by the state of your health and by your personal habits. The health and habits of your family members or friends may also affect your life and work. In the space below, list both positive and negative issues in this category. For example, you may have allergies that prevent you from working outdoors or in certain environments. On the other hand, you may enjoy the quality of good physical endurance that allows you to work in a physically demanding environment.

POSITIVES   NEGATIVES

_____   _____

_____   _____

_____   _____

_____   _____

Examine the positive elements. Are there some that you wish to continue, develop further, or protect?

_____

_____

_____

Now, examine the negative elements. Are there changes or adaptations that you can make to improve or solve those problems? Ideally, what would you like to see happen? Which of these elements can you change on your own? Start to develop a plan to address your concerns by filling in the blanks below.

My goals in the area of Health and Habits are to:

_____

_____

_____

_____

I can realistically begin to reach my goals by taking these steps:

1. _____

2. _____

3. _____

4. _____

5. _____

WORKSHEET 1.3
Family, Extended Family, and Friends

Your family, both immediate and extended, may present you with issues that assist or interfere with your life management. For example, if you are a parent of a young child or caregiver for an elderly parent, you must find a suitable caregiver during the hours that you work. Other issues affected by family concerns might include where you can work, the number of hours per day or week you can work, or whether you can travel for your job. In the space below, list the positive and negative factors in your personal relationships that affect your life and work.

POSITIVES   NEGATIVES

_____   _____

_____   _____

_____   _____

_____   _____

Examine the positive elements. Are there some that you wish to continue, develop further, or protect?

_____

_____

_____

Now, examine the negative elements. Are there changes or adaptations that you can make to improve or solve those problems? Ideally, what would you like to see happen? Which of these elements can you change on your own? Start to develop a plan to address your concerns by filling in the blanks below.

My goals in the area of Family, Extended Family, and Friends are to:

_____

_____

_____

_____

I can realistically begin to reach my goals by taking these steps:

1. _____

2. _____

3. _____

4. _____

5. _____

Career, Vocation, and Avocation

Your career or vocation (both can be terms for the work you do for a living) and your avocation (hobbies or work you do for fun or personal gratification) have an enormous impact on your life management. The majority of your waking hours are spent in work and hobbies. Your life management needs include finding a balance among the elements that demand your time and attention. In the area below, list the positive and negative aspects of your career, vocation, and avocation.

POSITIVES   NEGATIVES

_____   _____

_____   _____

_____   _____

_____   _____

Examine the positive elements. Are there some that you wish to continue, develop further, or protect?

_____

_____

_____

Now, examine the negative elements. Are there changes or adaptations that you can make to improve or solve these problems? Ideally, what would you like to see happen? Which of these elements can you change on your own? Start to develop a plan to address your concerns by filling in the blanks below.

My goals in the area of Career, Vocation, and Avocation are to:

_____

_____

_____

_____

I can realistically begin to reach my goals by taking these steps:

1. _____

2. _____

3. _____

4. _____

5. _____

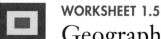

WORKSHEET 1.5

Geographic Location

Where you live and work can positively and negatively affect your life management plan. If you are physically close to family and friends in an area that is appealing to you, your location will have a positive effect on your life. Even so, climate or other physical conditions may negatively affect some elements of your life, for example, your commute time and conditions. List below all the aspects of your geographic location that affect your life, both positively and negatively.

POSITIVES   NEGATIVES

_____   _____

_____   _____

_____   _____

_____   _____

Examine the positive elements. Are there some that you wish to continue, develop further, or protect?

_____

_____

_____

Now, examine the negative elements. Are there changes or adaptations that you can make to improve or solve those problems? Ideally, what would you like to see happen? Which of these elements can you change on your own? Start to develop a plan to address your concerns by filling in the blanks below.

My goals in the area of Geographic Location are to:

_____

_____

_____

_____

I can realistically begin to reach my goals by taking these steps:

1. _____

2. _____

3. _____

4. _____

5. _____

Personal Growth and Development

The world has become a fast-changing environment with new discoveries and technologies appearing on an almost daily basis. The quality of your life and the quality of your work can be affected by your ability to understand and use new tools and information. On the chart below, list positive and negative aspects of your personal development, including education, training, knowledge, and experiences.

POSITIVES   NEGATIVES

_____   _____

_____   _____

_____   _____

_____   _____

_____   _____

Examine the positive elements. Are there some that you wish to continue, develop further, or protect?

_____

_____

_____

Now, examine the negative elements. Are there changes or adaptations that you can make to improve or solve those problems? Ideally, what would you like to see happen? Which of these elements can you change on your own? Start to develop a plan to address your concerns by filling in the blanks below.

My goals in the area of Personal Growth and Development are to:

_____

_____

_____

_____

I can realistically begin to reach my goals by taking these steps:

1. _____

2. _____

3. _____

4. _____

5. _____

Leisure and Recreation

Your body and mind need time to rest and recreate. Examine the time you have available for rest and recreation. What are the positive things that you do or that are available to you? List also the negative things affecting your leisure and recreation.

POSITIVES

NEGATIVES

_____   _____

_____   _____

_____   _____

_____   _____

_____   _____

Examine the positive elements. Are there some that you wish to continue, develop further, or protect?

_____

_____

_____

Now, examine the negative elements. Are there changes or adaptations that you can make to improve or solve those problems? Ideally, what would you like to see happen? Which of these elements can you change on your own? Start to develop a plan to address your concerns by filling in the blanks below.

My goals in the area of Leisure and Recreation are to:

_____

_____

_____

_____

I can realistically begin to reach my goals by taking these steps:

1. _____

2. _____

3. _____

4. _____

5. _____

Money Matters

Your personal finances, and the demands on those resources, have a strong influence on your life management. Each person has a different sense of his or her own needs and limits. Think about your financial situation. List the positives and negatives below.

POSITIVES

NEGATIVES

_____   _____

_____   _____

_____   _____

_____   _____

_____   _____

Examine the positive elements. Are there some that you wish to continue, develop further, or protect?

_____

_____

_____

Now, examine the negative elements. Are there changes or adaptations that you can make to improve or solve those problems? Ideally, what would you like to see happen? Which of these elements can you change on your own? Start to develop a plan to address your concerns by filling in the blanks below.

My goals in the area of Money Matters are to:

_____

_____

_____

_____

I can realistically begin to reach my goals by taking these steps:

1. _____

2. _____

3. _____

4. _____

5. _____

Wish List

As a final step in completing your life management plan, let's get creative and expansive. Think about what you would like to accomplish before you die. Don't look at your ideas critically; just write down desires that come to mind. This list can include knowledge or skills you'd like to learn, places you'd like to visit, experiences you'd like to have, and people you'd like to meet.

Wish List, or Things to Do Before I Die

EXAMPLES

- travel to Japan
- travel to Australia
- continue to be a loving family member and friend
- live in the Pacific Northwest on a houseboat for a summer
- write a book
- teach, work, or live in another country

Wish List:

_____

_____

_____

_____

_____

_____

_____

_____

_____

_____

_____

_____

_____

_____

_____

_____

Your Personal Mission Statement

After completing the exercises in the preceding section, you should now have a better sense of the motivating values and issues in your life that affect your career and job search. You can use this knowledge to build a vision of your purpose called your *personal mission statement*. Once you have defined this, you will have a better understanding of how to plan your journey through life. Look at the previous sections, and note the most important goals you have set for each aspect of life management.

LIFE MANAGEMENT AREAS   GOALS

Values   _____

                                    _____

Health and Habits   _____

                                    _____

Family, Extended Family, and Friends _____

                                    _____

Career, Vocation, and Avocation   _____

                                    _____

Geographic Location   _____

                                    _____

Personal Growth and Development   _____

                                    _____

Leisure and Recreation   _____

                                    _____

Money Matters   _____

                                    _____

Wish List   _____

                                    _____

PERSONAL MISSION STATEMENT

Keeping in mind your life management goals, write a personal mission statement reflecting the values and goals you have set for yourself. This statement can be as short or long as you like and should be unique to you. You may wish to include a statement about each of your goals, or concentrate on just a few key elements.

EXAMPLES

Janice had a very powerful, straightforward mission statement:

> *"To learn, to love, to be."*

Martha's mission statement is longer:

> *"To find work that I truly love; to make a positive contribution to my family and my community; to make the most of each and every day."*

Dan's mission statement is quite comprehensive:

> *"To live in harmony with nature and leave a legacy for my children. To maintain a healthy balance between work and family life.*
>
> *To use my talents, skills, and knowledge in work which is challenging and personally satisfying. To live in a place of natural beauty and help maintain it for generations to come.*
>
> *To continue to learn and grow and adapt to the changing world.*
>
> *To take regular time to engage in activities that will 'recreate' my mind and spirit.*
>
> *To make sufficient income to provide for my family's present and future needs, while being able to contribute time and money to causes in which I believe."*

Your Personal Mission Statement:

_____

_____

_____

_____

_____

_____

_____

_____

2

DEFINING YOUR IDEAL POSITION

There are many reasons why it is beneficial to have a well-defined job goal in mind, which we will call your "Ideal Position," as you progress through your job search. This Ideal Position changes at different stages of your life and career, making it important for you to assess its definition at each point of change or transition. First, your Ideal Position provides you with a goal and a direction. Second, it can be an asset in your networking efforts. And last, it is advantageous during the interview.

KNOWING YOUR IDEAL POSITION PROVIDES A GOAL AND DIRECTION

Many job seekers say, "I just want a job," implying that the specifics of the job are less important than finding a job. Well, if that were true, then any job would do for anyone. But, of course, that is not true, and there are many jobs that you would not want to have. Therefore, you must carefully define the specifications of your Ideal Position. A well-defined Ideal Position provides direction and parameters for a job search. Once you define your Ideal Position, then you can conduct research to identify those industries, organizations, and opportunities that potentially provide a perfect fit. You can develop or execute a job search plan to investigate opportunities.

KNOWING YOUR IDEAL POSITION AIDS IN YOUR NETWORKING EFFORTS

Many job seekers approach a network contact and simply state, "I am looking for a job and if you hear of anything, please let me know." There are very few people, even your closest friends or network contacts, who would know exactly what type of job situation would be ideal for you. To utilize your network effectively, you have to clearly communicate your Ideal Position. This includes such information as the type of position, industry, company, and location. Your network contact can be of more assistance to you if he or she has a clear picture of your intent. You will help your network members help you by doing your homework to define your Ideal Position.

KNOWING YOUR IDEAL POSITION PROVIDES CLARITY DURING THE INTERVIEW

Many job seekers find themselves unprepared when the interviewer asks, "Specifically, what type of job and company interests you?" or "Why are you interested in our company?" Having a well-articulated Ideal Position in mind prepares you to answer these kinds of questions with confidence.

DEFINING YOUR IDEAL POSITION

An Ideal Position is the integrated balance of five essential ingredients. These are:

- The Work Itself
- The Work Group and/or Boss
- The Organization
- The Industry
- The Geographic Location

Let's examine each of the five essential categories. Listed on the following pages are questions for you to answer under each category. This list is not meant to be all-inclusive, but instead serves as a starting point for your examination of your Ideal Position. There may be other elements that are important to you. Be sure to include them as well. If you are relatively inexperienced in the work force, think about school or community experiences you have had that can give you clues about your ideal preferences.

Picture yourself in the Ideal Position. Try to make your mental image rich in detail. Imagine how you look, what your surroundings are, what activities you are performing. Visualize your co-workers and your boss.

Now, answer each question with your thoughts about your Ideal Position. As you answer these questions, you may find it helpful to review your life management goals to make sure your Ideal Position is in harmony with your life choices.

The Work Itself

What are the functions and responsibilities?

_____

_____

_____

What is the authority level?

_____

_____

Do you have autonomy? Decision-making responsibilities?

_____

_____

_____

Do you work in a team or primarily alone?

_____

_____

Is there opportunity for advancement?

_____

_____

Will you be asked to develop and implement new ideas, programs, and/or campaigns?

_____

_____

_____

Does your work include travel? Relocation? What are the hours?

_____

_____

_____

Is the compensation and benefit plan competitive?

_____

_____

_____

Continued.

Does this job provide visibility within the organization, in the community, and among your professional peers?

_____

_____

In what ways will this job develop your ability to make a significant contribution to the company?

_____

_____

_____

What have been your biggest frustrations in your current or previous work experiences?

_____

_____

_____

Are the duties and responsibilities in line with your values, interests, and goals?

_____

_____

_____

The Work Group and/or Boss

What kind of work group or boss do you prefer? Supportive, encouraging? Someone who gives you free rein?

_____

_____

_____

Are your ideas received enthusiastically?

_____

_____

Is there an atmosphere of open communication?

_____

_____

_____

Do you receive acknowledgment and credit for your contributions?

_____

_____

_____

_____

What are the expectations, style, and chemistry of the working relationships?

_____

_____

_____

What is the boss's management or operating style?

_____

_____

_____

What are the values, priorities, and style of the boss or work group?

_____

_____

_____

What kind of decisions are you expected to bring to the boss to make?

_____

_____

_____

Do you prefer a hands-off or hands-on management style?

_____

_____

What have been your biggest frustrations with previous bosses or work groups?

_____

_____

_____

The Organization

Do you thrive in a small, medium-sized, or large organization?

_____

_____

What type of organization do you prefer? Public? Nonprofit? Family-owned?

_____

_____

Does the organization have a positive community image?

_____

_____

What are the organization's long-term objectives?

_____

_____

_____

What is the corporate culture?

_____

_____

_____

Describe the organizational structure that you prefer.

_____

_____

_____

Is the company competitive in the marketplace?

_____

_____

What are the company's sales and marketing strategies?

_____

_____

_____

Continued.

What are the company's principal products? Services? Potential new products or services?

_____

_____

_____

Who are the organization's chief competitors?

_____

_____

_____

What have been your biggest frustrations with previous organizations?

_____

_____

_____

What is the mission of the organization?

_____

_____

_____

The Industry

Where is this industry in the industrial life cycle? Growing? Maturing? Declining?

_____

_____

What industries have the most opportunities?

_____

_____

_____

What industries can use your skills?

_____

_____

How does the industry affect the quality of your work life?

_____

_____

What is the public image of the industry?

_____

_____

What are some related industries that might utilize your skills?

_____

_____

_____

What have been your biggest frustrations in your industry?

_____

_____

_____

Does the industry mesh with your values and interests?

_____

_____

_____

The Geographic Location

What are your climate preferences?

_____

_____

What is the local government like?

_____

_____

What types of services, recreation, entertainment, educational institutions, and shopping facilities are available in the community?

_____

_____

What is the cost of living and the social climate?

_____

_____

What types of housing are available?

_____

_____

What types of transportation and medical facilities are available?

_____

_____

How far are you willing to commute? In terms of miles or time?

_____

_____

Do you prefer to work in an urban, suburban, or rural location?

_____

_____

What have been some of your biggest frustrations with your current geographic location?

_____

_____

Ideal Position Worksheets

Use the following pages to complete *your Ideal Position* exercises. Under each category, define the elements that have created satisfaction for you in positions you have held. These elements can be described as *Positives*. From your list of positives, choose the ones that are the most important. These go on your *Must Have* list. Do this for each of the five categories, and then summarize the elements that create your composite Ideal Position.

Also list the components that are *Negatives*, and from this list choose the ones that you *Must Avoid*. The *must have* and the *must avoid* items will be helpful as you evaluate different opportunities during your job search. Also, if there are certain characteristics that you would like to see in your new position, list them as well.

The Work Itself

POSITIVES	MUST HAVE	NEGATIVES	MUST AVOID

What are the characteristics you would like to see in your new position?

(continued)

The Work Group and/or Boss

POSITIVES	MUST HAVE	NEGATIVES	MUST AVOID
_____	_____	_____	_____
_____	_____	_____	_____
_____	_____	_____	_____
_____	_____	_____	_____
_____	_____	_____	_____
_____	_____	_____	_____
_____	_____	_____	_____

What are the characteristics you would like to see in your new boss or work group?

_____

_____

_____

The Organization

POSITIVES	MUST HAVE	NEGATIVES	MUST AVOID
_____	_____	_____	_____
_____	_____	_____	_____
_____	_____	_____	_____
_____	_____	_____	_____
_____	_____	_____	_____
_____	_____	_____	_____

What are the characteristics you would like to see in your new organization?

_____

_____

_____

(continued)

The Industry

POSITIVES	MUST HAVE	NEGATIVES	MUST AVOID

What are the characteristics you would like to see in your industry?

_____

_____

_____

The Geographic Location

POSITIVES	MUST HAVE	NEGATIVES	MUST AVOID

What are the characteristics you would like to see in your geographic location?

_____

_____

_____

Ideal Position Summary

By reviewing and considering the Ideal Position exercises you have completed, you can now formulate a description of your Ideal Position. This description should include the position's job functions, reporting relationships, company profile, industrial makeup, and location. This description may continue to be refined and updated throughout your job search. This information is critical to your research and marketing efforts. Before you can implement a job search effectively, you need to be reasonably certain of your Ideal Position target.

The Work Itself

In my Ideal Position, I will be performing these activities:

_____

_____

The Work Group and/or Boss

In my Ideal Position, I will have co-workers and a manager/supervisor who are:

_____

_____

The Organization

In my Ideal Position, I will work for an organization that has these characteristics:

_____

_____

The Industry

In my Ideal Position, I will work in an industry that has these characteristics:

_____

_____

The Geographic Location

In my Ideal Position, I will be in a geographic setting that includes:

_____

_____

IDEAL POSITION EXAMPLES

Let's put the elements together and look at an example of an Ideal Position as constructed by Anne, a quality assurance technician. Anne had previously worked at a small company in the quality control field. She liked the field but felt that she had learned all that she could in her current employment situation. Also, she had a boss who was not encouraging her growth and development, an area which is very important to her. She defined her Ideal Position as working for a medium-sized company where she could be involved in a multitude of quality control efforts and learn from a professional work team. She also wanted a boss who would encourage her professional development. She was interested in continuing her education and wanted a company that would support her efforts. She was interested in working for a supplier to the automotive industry because she saw this industry as having great potential and continuously changing in its nature. She chose the metropolitan Detroit area as her geographic preference for both the opportunities in her area and quality of life. She enjoyed the four seasons and the recreational opportunities that the Great Lakes provided.

EXAMPLE 1

Another example of an Ideal Position is defined by John, an attorney. John had relocated with his executive wife and used the relocation as an opportunity to reflect on the direction of his life and career. He had worked for many years in a high-pressure environment with long hours. He decided that the quality of his life and spending time with his family were very important to him. His wife now had five weeks of vacation and they both loved to travel. John decided that the most important elements in his Ideal Position were flexibility, personal contribution, and a more relaxed atmosphere. He found a position with a small, growing computer software company that could use his expertise in the legal and operations area and allowed him to set a flexible 30-hour work week schedule with a generous (unpaid) vacation agreement. The position offered him exactly what he wanted and it was one where he could make a substantial contribution to the organization.

EXAMPLE 2

Finally, the third example of an Ideal Position is defined by Joseph, a graduating senior with a Bachelor of Science in Political Science. Joseph has a great love of sports, playing both hockey and baseball throughout his student career at a Division III school. While he knows he is not skilled enough to be a professional sports player in either sport, he would love to work for a professional sports team in some way. He worked his way through college as a summer counselor for a recreation program and organized a "Parents' Night Out" recreational program as a fundraising opportunity for his college teams. He also focused his senior project on professional players' organizations. After graduation, Joseph asked his coaches, professors, and parents' friends for referrals to managers of several semi-pro and professional teams in the Northeast. He was seeking a chance of working in marketing or management for the teams. He was successful in landing a part-time marketing job with a semi-pro hockey team, which led to a full-time opportunity within a year.

EXAMPLE 3

Your Ideal Position Summarized

Defining and Summarizing your Ideal Position gives you a starting point for your job search direction, research, prospecting, and networking efforts. You may add or augment elements as you proceed through your job search process. This exercise provides a framework to crystallize your thinking regarding what you find to be critical in your next job and helps to streamline your efforts. Knowing exactly what you are looking for can avoid unproductive tangents. Carefully defining your Ideal Position is a necessary step in taking charge of your future job and career success. Your Ideal Position is an important bridge between what you want and available jobs. Build this bridge carefully or you may feel like you're clinging to a rope bridge over a raging river chasm.

Summary of Ideal Position:

_____

_____

_____

_____

_____

_____

_____

_____

_____

_____

_____

_____

_____

_____

_____

_____

_____

_____

_____

_____

_____

3

SELF-ASSESSMENT AND BACKGROUND REVIEW

You've chosen your career destination by defining your Ideal Position. Now, you need to start planning the details of your trip, gathering the supporting information and documents, and assembling all of the items you'll need along the way. Your next step will be to review your background, examining your strengths, skills, interests, accomplishments, education and training, employment history, and professional activities. This examination will help you specifically target job opportunities that draw on your accumulated experiences and skills as well as fit your Ideal Position. This information will also be used to develop your resume, enable you to network more effectively, and prepare you to answer tough interview questions successfully.

On the following pages, complete the worksheets as thoroughly as possible. We have included some examples to help you, but the final words should be your own. As you work through the various exercises, you will begin to see a complete picture of your career emerge. Try to keep in mind your Ideal Position; use it as a guiding beacon. Choose those elements of your experience that best support your Ideal Position. Each of us has a multitude of skills, knowledge, and abilities that we can catalog; in this section, try to emphasize those that will move you closer to your destination.

You will complete worksheets covering the following topics:

Employment Summary
Skills Summary
Valued Skills
Action Verbs
Job Functions and Responsibilities
Accomplishments
Personal and Performance Qualities
Education Summary
Training Summary

Licenses and Certifications
Military Experience
Professional Memberships
Leadership Roles
Publications, Presentations, Languages
Volunteer and Community Activities
Hobbies, Interests
Career Summary

Employment Summary

The first step in the compilation of background information is to complete a summary sheet of all employers for which you have worked. For older workers, this listing does not need to go back further than 15–20 years. The Employer Summary sheet can be used in preparing your resume as well as in filling out applications for employment. Record the following information in chronological order, beginning with your first paid employer and continuing to your last or current employer.

FIRST EMPLOYER:

Dates Employed

Employer's Name

Address

Telephone Number

Job Title

Pay Rate or Salary

Supervisor's Name

Title _____ Dates _____

Other job titles held with this employer:

Title _____ Dates _____

Title _____ Dates _____

Title _____ Dates _____

(continued)

NEXT EMPLOYER:

Dates Employed _____

Employer's Name _____

Address _____

Telephone Number _____

Job Title _____

Pay Rate or Salary _____

Supervisor's Name _____

Title _____ Dates _____

Other job titles held with this employer:

Title _____ Dates _____

Title _____ Dates _____

Title _____ Dates _____

NEXT EMPLOYER:

Dates Employed _____

Employer's Name _____

Address _____

Telephone Number _____

Job Title _____

Pay Rate or Salary _____

Supervisor's Name _____

Title _____ Dates _____

Other job titles held with this employer:

Title _____ Dates _____

Title _____ Dates _____

Title _____ Dates _____

(continued)

NEXT EMPLOYER:

Dates Employed _____

Employer's Name _____

Address _____

Telephone Number _____

Job Title _____

Pay Rate or Salary _____

Supervisor's Name _____

Other job titles held with this employer:

Title _____ Dates _____

Title _____ Dates _____

Title _____ Dates _____

Title _____ Dates _____

NEXT EMPLOYER:

Dates Employed _____

Employer's Name _____

Address _____

Telephone Number _____

Job Title _____

Pay Rate or Salary _____

Supervisor's Name _____

Other job titles held with this employer:

Title _____ Dates _____

Title _____ Dates _____

Title _____ Dates _____

Title _____ Dates _____

Skills Summary

Listed below are categories of skills with accompanying action verbs. Think about skills that you have developed both through employment and through various community and civic activities.

Using the following scale, rate your ability level for each skill listed below.

1 = Highly skilled   2 = Moderately skilled   3 = Little or no skill

INTERPERSONAL SKILLS

_____ Guiding

_____ Counseling

_____ Communicating

_____ Listening

_____ Strengthening

_____ Influencing

_____ Persuading

_____ Moderating

_____ Cooperating

_____ Helping

_____ Understanding

_____ Mediating

_____ Selling

_____ Teaching

_____ Training

_____ Interviewing

_____ Negotiating

_____ Empathizing

_____ Acting as liaison

FOLLOW-THROUGH SKILLS

_____ Examining

_____ Proofreading

_____ Attending to details

_____ Recording

_____ Following directions

_____ Persisting

_____ Performing consistently

_____ Problem solving

_____ Evaluating

_____ Observing

_____ Computing

_____ Calculating

_____ Budgeting

_____ Researching

_____ Monitoring

_____ Estimating

MANUAL–PHYSICAL DEXTERITY SKILLS

_____ Building

_____ Repairing

_____ Restoring

_____ Manufacturing

_____ Sewing

_____ Cooking

_____ Typing

_____ Assembling

_____ Transporting

_____ Keeping fit

_____ Operating machinery

_____ Doing physical labor

_____ Planting

_____ Creating crafts

_____ Cultivating

_____ Caring for animals

_____ Using mechanical
abilities

_____ Nursing

(continued)

LEADERSHIP SKILLS

_____ Administering
_____ Managing
_____ Coaching
_____ Motivating
_____ Approving
_____ Directing
_____ Establishing
_____ Controlling
_____ Conducting
_____ Teaching
_____ Recruiting
_____ Decision making

ORGANIZATIONAL SKILLS

_____ Planning
_____ Scheduling
_____ Cataloging
_____ Arranging
_____ Sorting
_____ Indexing
_____ Prioritizing
_____ Systematizing
_____ Classifying
_____ Managing records
_____ Expediting
_____ Streamlining
_____ Coordinating
_____ Integrating

WRITING SKILLS

_____ Creating
_____ Drafting
_____ Compiling
_____ Analyzing
_____ Interpreting
_____ Summarizing
_____ Copying
_____ Revising
_____ Editing

CREATIVE SKILLS

_____ Inventing
_____ Developing
_____ Designing
_____ Experimenting
_____ Adapting
_____ Improving
_____ Imagining
_____ Visualizing
_____ Grasping ideas quickly
_____ Using intuition

ARTISTIC SKILLS

_____ Creating
_____ Sketching
_____ Painting
_____ Forming
_____ Using color
_____ Composing music
_____ Singing or playing music
_____ Appreciating aesthetics
_____ Dramatizing
_____ Entertaining
_____ Performing

Now, go back over your choices and circle those you would most like to use in your Ideal Position.

Valued Skills

The skills that you most enjoy using, and want to use in your next job, are your Valued Skills. They are the skills that require little effort on your part to use, because you are already moderately to highly competent in using them, and because you enjoy using them. You may also have circled some skills at which you are not yet competent, but that you wish to learn in your next job. Below, list the skills you chose in the appropriate section.

Highly skilled:

_____

_____

_____

_____

Moderately skilled:

_____

_____

_____

_____

Little to no skill:

_____

_____

_____

_____

Choose the skills that will be important in your Ideal Position.

_____

_____

_____

_____

_____

JOB FUNCTIONS AND RESPONSIBILITIES

You have completed your Employment Summary and have that information to refer to any time you need it in your resume development and job search process. Now we will begin to get more specific by examining the functions and responsibilities of your current and past jobs. Starting with your current job, you will determine your major duties and responsibilities within that job. You might begin this process by thinking of it as a circle or pie with three or four wedges comprising the major responsibilities of your jobs. What are those major functions? Under each major responsibility, you will have several duties that you regularly perform to see that the responsibility is met.

EXAMPLE 1

Employer: The Tofino Training Company
Job Title: Corporate Training Manager
Major Responsibility: Supervise trainers who conduct programs
Functions: Recruit, interview, and train staff
Perform annual performance reviews
Oversee staff development and education

Major Responsibility: Conduct needs assessment for management training
Functions: Go over management annual performance reviews
Review staffing needs
Conduct focus groups

Major Responsibility: Evaluate training programs
Functions: Go over staff performance reviews
Review course evaluations
Meet with trainers to discuss needs

EXAMPLE 2

Employer: The Olive Tree Restaurant
Job Title: Hostess
Major Responsibility: Greet and seat guests
Functions: Take phone reservations
Distribute guests equitably to accommodate wait staff
Provide menus

EXAMPLE 3

Employer: Ryder Automotive Engineering
Job Title: Engineering Supervisor
Major Responsibility: Assisted in the preparation of future vehicle test programs, vehicle shows, and engineering rides.
Duties: Ensured correct parts were installed
Arranged durability reviews and inspections
Maintained test fleet

ACTION VERBS

To get you started, look at the list of action verbs that are common to many job functions. Use these words to describe your primary duties and responsibilities. Check off all that apply to jobs that you have held. For example, if you checked the word *administer*, then describe your duty or responsibility beginning with the verb and completing the phrase with the action, for example: *administered the payroll for over 200 employees.*

_____ Achieved	_____ Briefed	_____ Controlled	_____ Effected
_____ Acquired	_____ Budgeted	_____ Coordinated	_____ Eliminated
_____ Adjusted	_____ Built	_____ Corrected	_____ Employed
_____ Administered	_____ Calculated	_____ Counseled	_____ Encouraged
_____ Advised	_____ Cataloged	_____ Counted	_____ Enlarged
_____ Aided	_____ Changed	_____ Created	_____ Enrolled
_____ Analyzed	_____ Checked	_____ Critiqued	_____ Ensured
_____ Anticipated	_____ Cited	_____ Defined	_____ Established
_____ Applied	_____ Classified	_____ Delegated	_____ Evaluated
_____ Appointed	_____ Closed	_____ Delivered	_____ Examined
_____ Appraised	_____ Commanded	_____ Demonstrated	_____ Excelled
_____ Approved	_____ Communicated	_____ Deployed	_____ Executed
_____ Arbitrated	_____ Compared	_____ Designed	_____ Expanded
_____ Arranged	_____ Completed	_____ Determined	_____ Expedited
_____ Assembled	_____ Composed	_____ Developed	_____ Familiarized
_____ Assessed	_____ Computed	_____ Devised	_____ Financed
_____ Assisted	_____ Conceived	_____ Diagnosed	_____ Formulated
_____ Assumed	_____ Concluded	_____ Directed	_____ Forwarded
_____ Attended	_____ Conducted	_____ Disapproved	_____ Fostered
_____ Audited	_____ Consolidated	_____ Discovered	_____ Found
_____ Authored	_____ Constructed	_____ Distributed	_____ Gained
_____ Authorized	_____ Consulted	_____ Documented	_____ Gathered
_____ Awarded	_____ Contracted	_____ Earned	_____ Governed
_____ Bought	_____ Contributed	_____ Edited	_____ Graded

_____ Grossed	_____ Made	_____ Programmed	_____ Solved
_____ Grouped	_____ Maintained	_____ Projected	_____ Specialized
_____ Guided	_____ Managed	_____ Promoted	_____ Specified
_____ Handled	_____ Matched	_____ Purchased	_____ Stated
_____ Helped	_____ Maximized	_____ Qualified	_____ Streamlined
_____ Hired	_____ Minimized	_____ Rated	_____ Strengthened
_____ Housed	_____ Moderated	_____ Received	_____ Studied
_____ Identified	_____ Modified	_____ Recommended	_____ Submitted
_____ Implemented	_____ Monitored	_____ Recorded	_____ Suggested
_____ Improved	_____ Motivated	_____ Recruited	_____ Summarized
_____ Included	_____ Negotiated	_____ Rectified	_____ Supervised
_____ Incorporated	_____ Netted	_____ Reduced	_____ Surveyed
_____ Increased	_____ Observed	_____ Reported	_____ Systematized
_____ Indexed	_____ Operated	_____ Researched	_____ Targeted
_____ Initiated	_____ Ordered	_____ Reshaped	_____ Taught
_____ Inspected	_____ Organized	_____ Resolved	_____ Tested
_____ Instructed	_____ Originated	_____ Returned	_____ Toured
_____ Interviewed	_____ Oversaw	_____ Reviewed	_____ Tracked
_____ Introduced	_____ Participated	_____ Revised	_____ Trained
_____ Invented	_____ Perceived	_____ Saved	_____ Transformed
_____ Inventoried	_____ Performed	_____ Scheduled	_____ Translated
_____ Investigated	_____ Persuaded	_____ Screened	_____ Wrote
_____ Issued	_____ Pioneered	_____ Scrutinized	
_____ Joined	_____ Planned	_____ Selected	
_____ Laid out	_____ Prepared	_____ Served	
_____ Launched	_____ Presented	_____ Serviced	
_____ Lectured	_____ Presided	_____ Shipped	
_____ Led	_____ Processed	_____ Showed	
_____ Located	_____ Produced	_____ Simplified	

Job Functions and Responsibilities

Next, go through your list of Action Verbs and list your current job functions, including your daily activities. Below, list these under your three or four major responsibilities. At this time, leave the Accomplishments column blank, as you will fill in that information later.

After you list the responsibilities and functions for your current job, list them for your prior positions; do this in reverse chronological order, beginning with your most recent job, then working backward in time.

Current Job

Employer: _____

City, State: _____

Job Title: _____

Dates This Job Held: _____

Major Responsibility: _____

_____

FUNCTIONS: ACCOMPLISHMENTS:

_____   _____

_____   _____

_____   _____

_____   _____

Major Responsibility: _____

_____

FUNCTIONS: ACCOMPLISHMENTS:

_____   _____

_____   _____

_____   _____

_____   _____

Look at your list of functions and eliminate ones that are less important. Look to see where there are redundancies. Also look at areas that can be logically grouped together. Next, number them in order of importance to you with the most important as number 1.

(continued)

Prior Job

Employer: _____

City, State: _____

Job Title: _____

Dates This Job Held: _____

Major Responsibility: _____

_____

FUNCTIONS: ACCOMPLISHMENTS:

_____   _____

_____   _____

_____   _____

_____   _____

_____   _____

_____   _____

Major Responsibility: _____

_____

FUNCTIONS: ACCOMPLISHMENTS:

_____   _____

_____   _____

_____   _____

_____   _____

_____   _____

(continued)

Prior Job

Employer: _____

City, State: _____

Job Title: _____

Dates This Job Held: _____

Major Responsibility: _____

_____

FUNCTIONS: ACCOMPLISHMENTS:

_____   _____

_____   _____

_____   _____

_____   _____

_____   _____

_____   _____

Major Responsibility: _____

_____

FUNCTIONS: ACCOMPLISHMENTS:

_____   _____

_____   _____

_____   _____

_____   _____

_____   _____

(continued)

45

Prior Job

Employer: _____

City, State: _____

Job Title: _____

Dates This Job Held: _____

Major Responsibility: _____

_____

FUNCTIONS: ACCOMPLISHMENTS:

_____   _____

_____   _____

_____   _____

_____   _____

_____   _____

_____   _____

Major Responsibility: _____

_____

FUNCTIONS: ACCOMPLISHMENTS:

_____   _____

_____   _____

_____   _____

_____   _____

_____   _____

_____   _____

For each of the prior jobs you've listed, go back and review your list of functions. Eliminate ones that are less important. Look to see where there are redundancies. Also look at areas that can be logically grouped together. Next, number them in order of importance to you with the most important as number 1.

ACCOMPLISHMENTS

No one ever performs a job exactly like another person would. You bring to your work your sense of values, priorities, and your personal strengths, all of which influence how and why you do the job the way you do. As you performed your job, you probably set goals, either in conjunction with your supervisor or within your own framework, according to what you knew had to be done. Reaching a goal is an accomplishment. It is also an accomplishment to strive to meet a goal, even if external factors prevent you from achieving what you had hoped. You can also feel a sense of accomplishment from knowing that you performed at the best of your ability, learned something new, or overcame some obstacle. Finally, if your supervisor or employer recognizes your performance as superior, that is an accomplishment. Your accomplishments will be as unique as you are.

Go back to your descriptions of the preceding job titles. To the right of the duty and responsibility information that you've already answered, list some of your major accomplishments. One good way to get started is to remember: Problems, Solutions, Results. What *problems* did you face in your job? What *actions* did you take to solve the problems? Finally, what was the *result* of those solutions? The result is your accomplishment. Whenever possible, try to *quantify* the impact your accomplishment had on the company. For example, *"Increased production of widgets by 35 percent through process and equipment improvements,"* or *"Decreased overtime by 15 percent and increased productivity by 25 percent through job redesign."*

MORE EXAMPLES OF ACCOMPLISHMENTS

- Received Community Spirit Award in 1996.
- Designed and implemented several policies and procedures for increasing departmental accuracy.
- Authored IBM-based cost accounting software for the application of domestic and international purchasing resulting in a 300 percent increase in efficiency.
- Viewed by administrative sales staff as demonstrating strong leadership, excellent communication skills, and ability to gain rapport quickly with clients.
- Financed 100 percent of college costs through summer jobs, work-study, and student loans.
- Led fund-raising drive for elementary school playground, achieving 110 percent of goal within a six-month period.

After listing your accomplishments, go back over them. Within each job, prioritize them in order of importance to you in terms of presenting yourself for a new position. As with your skills, you may have achieved some wonderful accomplishments by facing problems that you hope never to see again. Other accomplishments may have resulted from the kind of problems that you enjoy facing and solving. Indicate priority by using 1 for the most important, 2 for the next, and so on.

After you have prioritized the accomplishments within each job, look at them in terms of your total work history. Choose at least five of the top-rated accomplishments overall that show your ability to have a positive impact with an employer, focusing on those that directly support your next Ideal Position.

Summarize your five top-rated (key) accomplishments below:

1. _____

_____

_____

2. _____

_____

_____

3. _____

_____

_____

4. _____

_____

_____

5. _____

_____

_____

Personal and Performance Qualities Checklist

As with accomplishments, you possess a unique set of personal qualities that influence how you do your work. Employers often make hiring decisions based partly on these qualities. For example, an accounting firm will want to hire accountants who are thorough, precise, and good at communicating complex information to others. The next exercise will help you inventory the personal and performance qualities that you possess, and then prioritize them in terms of importance to your desired job.

Check each term that you feel describes you.

_____ Accurate	_____ Deliberate	_____ Industrious
_____ Active	_____ Dependable	_____ Informal
_____ Adaptable	_____ Dignified	_____ Intellectual
_____ Adventuresome	_____ Discreet	_____ Introspective
_____ Ambitious	_____ Dominant	_____ Inventive
_____ Analytical	_____ Eager	_____ Kind
_____ Artistic	_____ Easygoing	_____ Likable
_____ Assertive	_____ Efficient	_____ Logical
_____ Broad-minded	_____ Emotional	_____ Loves learning
_____ Businesslike	_____ Emphasis on quality	_____ Loyal
_____ Calm	_____ Energetic	_____ Mature
_____ Capable	_____ Enthusiastic	_____ Methodical
_____ Careful	_____ Fair-minded	_____ Meticulous
_____ Cautious	_____ Firm	_____ Motivated
_____ Clear goals	_____ Flexible	_____ Open-minded
_____ Clear thinking	_____ Formal	_____ Organized
_____ Communicates clearly	_____ Frank	_____ Original
_____ Competent	_____ Friendly	_____ Outgoing
_____ Confident	_____ Goal-directed	_____ Patient
_____ Considerate	_____ Good appearance	_____ Persistent
_____ Conscientious	_____ Good-natured	_____ Persuasive
_____ Consistent	_____ Healthy	_____ Physically fit
_____ Cooperative	_____ Helpful	_____ Pleasant
_____ Creative	_____ Honest	_____ Poised
_____ Curious	_____ Idealistic	_____ Polite
_____ Decisive	_____ Imaginative	_____ Positive attitude
_____ Dedicated	_____ Independent	_____ Practical

(continued)

_____ Precise	_____ Sense of humor	_____ Timely
_____ Problem-solving abilities	_____ Sensible	_____ Tolerant
_____ Progressive	_____ Sensitive	_____ Trusting
_____ Punctual	_____ Serious	_____ Trustworthy
_____ Purposeful	_____ Service-oriented	_____ Unassuming
_____ Quick	_____ Sincere	_____ Understanding
_____ Quiet	_____ Sociable	_____ Verbal
_____ Rational	_____ Spontaneous	_____ Versatile
_____ Reflective	_____ Stable	_____ Wise
_____ Relaxed	_____ Steady	_____ Witty
_____ Reliable	_____ Strong	_____ Works intelligently
_____ Resourceful	_____ Supportive	_____ Works well alone
_____ Responsible	_____ Sympathetic	_____ Works well in groups or teams
_____ Rises to new challenges	_____ Tactful	_____ Works well under pressure
_____ Self-disciplined	_____ Takes pride in work	
_____ Self-starter	_____ Tenacious	
	_____ Thorough	

Now go back through the list and circle 10 to 20 qualities that you consider to be your strongest. List them below.

_____

_____

_____

_____

_____

_____

_____

Which of these traits are necessary to be successful in your Ideal Position?

_____

_____

_____

_____

Additional Information

Now you are going to complete your information on education, training, certification and licenses, and military experience.

Education Summary

SCHOOL NAME _____

Dates Attended _____

Course of Study/Major and Minor _____

Degree or Certificate _____

Honors/Awards _____

Key Courses Completed _____

_____

_____

_____

Achievements/Clubs/Other Activities _____

_____

_____

SCHOOL NAME _____

Dates Attended _____

Course of Study/Major and Minor _____

Degree or Certificate _____

Honors/Awards _____

Key Courses Completed _____

_____

_____

_____

Achievements/Clubs/Other Activities _____

_____

_____

(continued)

Training Summary

In-House Training Programs _____
_____
_____

Professionally Certified Training _____
_____
_____

Professional Development Conferences or Seminars _____
_____
_____

Licenses and Certifications

License/Certificate _____   License/Certificate _____

Issuing Agent _____   Issuing Agent _____

License Number _____   License Number _____

Issue Date _____   Issue Date _____

Expiration Date _____   Expiration Date _____

Military Experience

Branch _____

Location _____

Rank _____

Special Training _____
_____
_____
_____

Honors/Awards _____
_____

(continued)

Professional Memberships

_____

_____

Leadership Roles

_____

_____

Publications

_____

_____

Presentations

_____

_____

Languages

_____

_____

Community Activities

_____

_____

Volunteer Activities

_____

_____

Hobbies, Interests

_____

_____

CAREER SUMMARY

Your final step is to develop a career or qualifications summary. This summary is an overview of your background and experience. It can be used on your resume as an introduction and is useful during networking conversations or during the interview. To begin, write three sentences that describe what you want an employer to know about you. Include statements regarding skills, experience, or personal qualities. This statement will probably need to be written and revised several times. Don't give up. Keep working on it until you have a well-written, concise summary of the important facets of your background and career that you want to convey.

EXAMPLE 1

Over 20 years of experience in product manufacturing and automotive technical field. Areas of expertise include electrical, electronic, and mechanical analysis and diagnosis of faulty vehicles and production-related equipment. Familiar with the repair of pneumatic and hydraulic processes; able to read blueprints and hydraulic and electrical schematics and perform computer diagnostic tests.

EXAMPLE 2

Highly motivated manager with solid analytical background and comprehensive experience in the manufacture of food. Areas of experience include management, statistics, administration, process reengineering and dealing with regulatory agencies. Strong PC skills including Lotus 1-2-3, Excel, Microsoft Word, Genesis, and Fourth Shift.

EXAMPLE 3

Over seven years' experience in a counseling capacity working primarily with parolees; physically, mentally, and emotionally impaired young adults; and senior citizens confined to their homes. Skilled in initial assessments, formulating a remedial plan, and connecting clients with appropriate area resources.

EXAMPLE 4

Over ten years' experience in customer relations. Areas of expertise include customer education and communication, special projects, product research, and PC and mainframe capability. Proficient in Word for Windows, Excel, PowerPoint and Microsoft Access.

EXAMPLE 5

Highly motivated graduate with extensive coursework and internship experience in social science programs. BA in Sociology, demonstrated skills in one-on-one counseling and group presentation skills. Proficiency in Microsoft Office and Internet applications.

EXAMPLE 6

Proven leader with strong management and administrative skills. Skilled in managing budgets, complex projects, and people.

Career Summary:

_____

_____

_____

_____

_____

_____

_____

_____

_____

4
WRITING
YOUR RESUME

As you begin writing your resume, let's review the definition of a resume.

Resume: 1. A summary, especially a brief, written presentation, of one's employment or professional history and educational background submitted to employers. 2. A document that communicates one's career interest and experience in a clear, concise manner. 3. A document that demonstrates one's abilities, accomplishments, and education. 4. A document reviewed by employers prior to granting interviews. 5. A marketing tool to stimulate an employer's interest.

When you look at all of the information that you pulled together for the last section, you probably are impressed with the amount of data you have gathered describing you and your background. It is like packing for a kayaking trip: you always seem to have more gear than you need. If you were packing for such a trip, you would probably lay your gear out on the living room floor and carefully decide what is necessary to bring. Now that you have all of your background "gear" or information gathered, you need to review it carefully and select only the information that is most important for you to convey about yourself to a prospective employer. As you do this, also keep in mind your Ideal Position. You want your resume to mesh with your Ideal Position as much as possible.

You may want to use a yellow highlighter to mark those critical items that you want to be sure to include in your resume. At the end of this section is a resume worksheet. Draft a copy of your resume, using the information from the self-assessment and background review section. Most resumes take several drafts, so don't be disappointed if it isn't perfect after the first draft. Let your resume sit overnight and then come back to it the next day.

Following the resume draft worksheet section, we have included a section entitled "A Resume Check—Does your Resume Measure Up?" You may want to refer to this section as you proceed with your resume draft. Following the resume check is a section with numerous sample resumes. Take time to study this section as well. We suggest that you use your highlighter to mark the resumes that you like. We have included resumes from different fields and industries as well as different formats.

TYPES OF RESUMES

Chronological

A chronological resume is written according to date, in reverse order, so that the most recent position appears at the beginning of the resume with prior employment following. This format is commonly used by resume writers and is often preferred by employers. It works well for someone who has had a steady career progression through similar jobs and who is targeting the next logical position.

Functional

A functional resume is written to emphasize job functions and de-emphasize dates and employers. Skills and accomplishments are grouped under functional headings, such as "Sales Experience" or "Management Experience." It is best used by people who are new to the work force, who are making a career change, or who have gaps in their work history. If you choose this format, you can include a brief chronological employment history section at the end to satisfy employers who want to clearly see your career progression.

Prioritized

A prioritized resume is written with the most important work experience first. Dates may be left off. This format may be used when the position that you are seeking is different from your most recent employment and you have had other past experience which more closely matches.

As you can quickly see, there are no hard and fast rules when it comes to writing your resume. There *are* guidelines and, within these, you have room to make your resume truly a reflection of you and your strengths, accomplishments, experiences, and education. Choose the format that works best for you.

WHAT TO INCLUDE

When developing a resume, it is important to keep in mind that one size or format does not fit all job seekers. However, there are some typical categories of information that are commonly used on resumes. These include:

Heading. The heading consists of your name, address, and phone number. This information is generally centered and placed at the top of the resume.

Career summary. This is usually a short paragraph providing a broad overview of experience, accomplishments, length of time in your field, and possibly some professional attributes. Be sure that it is a well-written compilation of your career, background, and abilities.

Professional or employment history. This section can be presented in a chronological, functional, or prioritized format. The chronological format is most commonly used. It offers a listing of your experience and accomplishments in reverse chronological order, starting with your most recent job. This format emphasizes titles and organizations. If you have decided that a chronological resume is best for you, are your jobs listed in reverse chronological order (with most recent job first)?

The functional resume emphasizes job functions and categories of abilities. In this format, the job titles, work history, and employing companies are given less emphasis. If you write a functional resume, describe clearly and succinctly your work experience and job functions. Include information on the type, size, product, and industry of the companies at which you have worked. (A prospective employer may not be familiar with the company name.)

Emphasize your accomplishments demonstrating your problem-solving abilities. List your functions and accomplishments in order of importance. Include information on your work habits, attitudes, and communication abilities.

Education. In this section, list college courses, degrees, and relevant job or other specialized training that you have completed. If you have attended college, it is usually not necessary to list your high school education. Include any special proficiencies that you may have, such as an ability to use computers and various software programs.

Military experience. If you were in the military, provide a brief description of your service.

Professional affiliations. Do you belong to or serve on a board for a professional organization in your field or industry? If so, include this information.

Community or volunteer work. Are you involved with community or volunteer work that would be impressive to a prospective employer? If so, list it.

Hobbies and interests. This section may be inserted or omitted depending on the significance of the information. If it helps to present a more positive image, then include it.

Now let's look at the layout of the information on your resume.

LAYOUT

Generally speaking, employers prefer a one-page resume. Two pages are acceptable if the most important information appears on the first page.

Use a quality paper stock for reproducing your resume. Your local office supply store will carry a variety of resume stock papers and envelopes in various colors and weights. Choose a neutral color such as white or off white.

Don't include your references on your resume. List them on a separate sheet of matching paper to be provided at or after the interview when requested by the interviewer.

Resume Draft Worksheet

Name _____

Address _____

Phone Number _____

Fax _____ E-Mail _____

Qualifications or Career Summary

Complete this section using information from your self-assessment exercises. You might include skills, personal qualities, values, and/or knowledge areas. Everything included should support your Ideal Position target. See the resume examples that follow the worksheet to get ideas on how to structure your Summary.

_____

_____

_____

_____

_____

_____

_____

Employment or Professional History (for chronological format)

Organization _____

Job Title _____

Brief description of duties and responsibilities _____

_____

_____

_____

_____

Accomplishments _____

_____

_____

_____

OR

(continued)

Job Function or Most Important Work Experience
(for functional or prioritized resume)

_____

_____

_____

Accomplishments _____

_____

_____

Employment or Professional History (for chronological format)

Organization _____

Job Title _____

Brief description of duties and responsibilities _____

_____

_____

_____

_____

_____

Accomplishments _____

_____

_____

OR

Job Function or Most Important Work Experience
(for functional or prioritized resume)

_____

_____

_____

Accomplishments _____

_____

_____

(continued)

Continued.

Employment or Professional History (for chronological format)

Organization _____

Job Title _____

Brief description of duties and responsibilities _____

_____

_____

_____

Accomplishments _____

_____

_____

OR

Job Function or Most Important Work Experience (for functional or prioritized resume)

_____

_____

_____

Accomplishments _____

_____

_____

Employment or Professional History (for chronological format)

Organization _____

Job Title _____

Brief description of duties and responsibilities _____

_____

_____

_____

Accomplishments _____

_____

_____

OR

(continued)

Job Function or Most Important Work Experience
(for functional or prioritized resume)

_____

_____

_____

Accomplishments _____

_____

_____

Education

_____

_____

_____

Training

_____

_____

_____

Licenses, Certifications

_____

_____

Honors, Awards

_____

_____

Military Experience

_____

_____

(continued)

Professional Affiliations

_____

_____

Community and Volunteer Work

_____

_____

_____

Hobbies and Interests (do not include unless very relevant to job)

_____

_____

Special Skills or Qualifications

_____

_____

_____

Using the Resume Draft Worksheet and the resume samples for examples, now you'll put your resume into printed form. Your first step is to determine which format serves you best—chronological, functional, or prioritized. After you select the format, decide how to organize and present the information you summarized on the Resume Draft Worksheet. Don't be concerned if this takes several attempts before you are satisfied. Finally, read the next section, "Does Your Resume Measure Up?" and check your resume to determine if any final changes need to be made. Make any necessary changes and finalize your resume.

Does Your Resume Measure Up?

Now that you have spent many hours developing and writing your resume, it is time to put it to a final test. Use this Resume Check to ensure that you have covered all of the bases. Once your resume has met your final critique, you should be ready to sail away on your job search.

Tape your resume to the wall, stand back, and take a critical look at its visual appearance. Ask yourself:

How does it look? Too cluttered? Too much white space?

Is it balanced? Attractive? Do your headings stand out?

Have you used CAPITALIZATION, underlining, different size fonts, **bold face type**, and *italics* to highlight headings and important information?

Have you used these techniques consistently and attractively?

Does your resume present a businesslike, professional appearance?

Overall Checks—Do's and Don'ts

Do's

- Thoroughly eliminate the "Typo Devil" from your resume. Watch out; errors are extremely difficult to find. Have another person review it as well.
- Use your computer word processing software tools, such as spell check and grammar check. Remember, spell check will not pick up errors in which the word is correctly spelled but incorrect in the context in which you are using it. For example, "fore years of college."
- Begin your sentences with action verbs to give them impact and keep them succinct. Avoid using the word "I" to describe your functions and accomplishments.
- Include "Willing to Relocate" if you are looking for a job outside of your geographic area.

Don'ts

- Don't include any unrelated or irrelevant employment. Have you gone back too far chronologically? Usually, a resume does not need to cover more than 10–15 years.
- Don't use too much specialized jargon or many abbreviations. Remember, your resume may be read by individuals who are not familiar with your particular niche. For example, it may be read by the human resources professional, who is not necessarily familiar with highly technical computer systems jargon.
- Don't include personal data such as height, weight, marital status, or number of children.

Your resume is an important tool for your job-seeking efforts. Use this Resume Check to give your resume a final critique. You should now be ready to develop your job search plan.

RESUME EXAMPLES

On the following pages are numerous examples of resumes from people in many different fields, representing each type of resume format. Use these for ideas, as well as for formatting and organizing information.

SAMANTHA A. ANCEL
3375 S. Alphabet Circle
Hartland Hills, MS 80126
(405) 843-5241

CAREER SUMMARY
Over seven years' experience in customer relations. Areas of expertise include customer education and communication, special projects, product research, and PC and mainframe capability in Word for Windows, Excel, PowerPoint, and Microsoft Access.

PROFESSIONAL EXPERIENCE
SPORTS AND ENTERTAINMENT CENTER, Arlington Hills, MS, 1995–present

Account Representative
Primarily responsible for selling, serving and expanding ticket sales for major sports events, concerts, family shows and special entertainment packages. Handle ticket sales for basketball, soccer and hockey events involving corporate, group and individual sales. Resolve problems, special issues and complaints involving ticket sales and events.

- Sold the most Merchant Night Packages among sales staff of eight.
- Viewed by administrative sales staff as demonstrating strong leadership, excellent communication skills, and ability to gain rapport quickly with clients.

PACKARD MOTOR DIVISION, Warren, MS, 1994–1995

Vehicle Operations Manager, Communications
Assisted in planning of full product line preview and other events involving over 100 vehicles. Responded to journalist's requests involving information on past, current and future vehicle models. Worked with Packard Motor Division and Quality Corp. to order new fleet vehicles. Handled departmental communications concerning vehicle issues and programs.

- Developed a computerized internal tracking system utilizing Microsoft Access to monitor over 200 vehicles evaluated and used by members of the media.

MIS, Troy, MS, 1990–1993

Information Center Manager
Responded to journalists' communication inquiries concerning products, sales figures, and programs. Represented Communications at press events. Assisted in the development of an exhibit at the Heritage Showcase. Updated and wrote biographies of various executives.

Service Relations Analyst
- Researched and answered customer questions concerning product features and availability of options. Involved with special projects including 1993 Customer Assistance Center Product Walk-A-Rounds and Visions: The Women's Expo in Dulles, Mississippi.
- Developed support material for various activities and functions.
- Trained new employees concerning procedures, communication skills and computer systems. Served as Team Manager when the manager was not available.
- Communicated position on various issues and product information to current and prospective owners. Resolved issues with owners and dealers.

EDUCATION
Butler University, Indianapolis, IN
Bachelor of Science in Radio and Television. Minor: Business Administration
Graduated *Cum Laude,* GPA 3.8.

JONATHON M. BERGSTROM

235 Danbury Road   Saratoga Springs, NY 12688   518-538-6372

JOB OBJECTIVE: A position in sports management.

PERSONAL & PROFESSIONAL QUALITIES:

- Demonstrated ability to accept responsibility and risks.
- Able to work independently or as team member.
- Excellent interpersonal skills; can handle conflict constructively.

EDUCATION:

SKIDMORE COLLEGE, Saratoga Springs, NY

         Bachelor of Arts in Government   1997

       Studies include: Independent Study—*Anti-trust and Free Agency Laws in Baseball*

         Business Law I and II   Sport and Social Issues

         Business Ethics and Society   Sport Psychology

BERKSHIRE PREPARATORY SCHOOL, Sheffield, MA   1993

SARATOGA SPRINGS HIGH SCHOOL, Saratoga Springs, NY   1992

WORK HISTORY:

SIRO'S RESTAURANT, Saratoga Springs, NY   1989 to 1996

     World-class restaurant open only during racing season, serving 220 to 380 dinners per night.

     Expediter (1994 to 1996)

         Directed and maintained pace and priority in kitchen to assure timely and correct delivery of customers' orders. Selected for position; learned on the job. Reported to Executive Chef.

- Received orders from wait staff; called out orders to chefs for initial and final preparation.
- Tracked timing and progress of orders; finished off orders and delivered plates to wait staff.
- Hired, scheduled, and disciplined dishwashing staff.
- Assisted with daily kitchen preparations.

     Prep Cook (1993)

     Dishwasher (1989 to 1992)

SARATOGA SPRINGS RECREATION COMMISSION, Saratoga Springs, NY   1994 to 1996

     Community recreation program provider.

     Baseball Clinic Coordinator (1996)

         Coordinated 5-day baseball skill instruction clinic for youth ages 7 to 14 years. Supervised instructors and planned daily drills, exercises, and activities.

     Baseball Clinic Instructor (1994, 1995)

UNION COLLEGE HOCKEY CLINIC, Schenectady, NY   1990

     Instructor

OTHER ACTIVITIES:

KIDS' NIGHT OUT, Skidmore College   1993 to 1997

     Fundraising activity for Skidmore Baseball Team providing 4-hour supervised activities in the college athletic facility for local youth ages 6 to 14.

         Organizer

            Set up facility, scheduled and supervised monitors, maintained discipline.

SKIDMORE COLLEGE BASEBALL TEAM, New York State Division III   1993 to 1997

     Team Captain (1996, 1997)

SKIDMORE COLLEGE HOCKEY TEAM, New York State Division III   1993 to 1997

68

PAUL G. CARRINGTON
825 Ashley Drive
Decatur, GA 30342
(404) 598-4567

CAREER SUMMARY

Approximately five years' experience in a counseling capacity working primarily with parolees, physically, mentally and emotionally impaired young adults, and senior citizens confined to their homes. Skilled in initial assessments, formulating a remedial plan, and connecting clients with appropriate area resources.

PROFESSIONAL EXPERIENCE

SOUTH ATLANTA PAROLE OFFICE, Atlanta, GA
1994–1998
Parole Officer II

Counseled up to 100 parolees at any given time. Conducted initial assessment to determine a case plan of action. Decided on specific course of treatment, which may have included drug/alcohol counseling, referral to vocational rehabilitation, job training, educational training, and medical treatment. Responsible for enrolling or encouraging entrance into proper treatment or medical programs. Coordinated with referring agencies to initiate services. Completed delinquent reports, quarterly assessments, legal, background, and social investigations. Periodically presented cases to Parole Board. Conducted regular follow-up visits with parolees to check and monitor case plan progress. Verified employment and residence.

- Regularly maintained between 90% to 100% of the required contact with each parolee on a monthly basis.
- Consistently produced accurate and on-time required reports.
- Viewed by management staff as being conscientious, well organized, working well under pressure, dependable, and resourceful.

NATIONAL CRISIS INTERVENTION, Carmine, FL
1993–1994
Crisis Intervention Counselor

Conducted telephone counseling at a community-funded crisis center. Counseled mentally and emotionally impaired college students, chronic dysfunctional personalities, and senior adults. Focused on issues ranging from drug use, suicide, and situational crises to stress, paranoia, and similar problems. Referred clients to proper local resources.

EDUCATION

Southern Illinois University, Carbondale, IL
Bachelor of Science: Criminal Justice
Concentration in Administration of Justice
Minor: Psychology

JENNIE BOWSER
567 Pine Court
Green Mountain, NY 12498
(518) 937-2745

OBJECTIVE:

Sales/Sales Management with potential for growth and advancement.

HIGHLIGHTS of QUALIFICATIONS:

- 7 years of retail service and sales in high customer contact settings.
- 3 years demonstrated success in sales management.
- Excellent ability to motivate, train, and supervise staff.
- Extensive merchandise set-up, display, and promotional experience.
- Excellent problem-solving ability and focus on sales and customer service.
- High energy, outgoing, honest, trustworthy, and loyal employee.

SALES and SALES MANAGEMENT EXPERIENCE:

NUTRI/SYSTEM, Schenectady, NY   1993 to 1998

Center Manager (1995–1998) Promoted from Team Leader. Overall accountability for Center operations and profitability. Maintained computerized inventory control and cost of goods system. Hired, trained, and supervised staff. Conducted and closed initial sales meeting with clients. Met with clients as Personal Consultant as needed.

- Increased client base and revenues through telemarketing efforts to former clients.
- Held daily meetings with staff to set goals, solve problems, and improve motivation.
- Maintained percent of Payroll to Revenue below company standards.
- Created and set-up posters and displays to promote products and services.
- Consistently met company and/or personal sales goals prior to downsizing.

Team Leader (1993–1995) Promoted from Personal Consultant. Oversaw staff of up to five Personal Consultants and consulted with clients as needed. Reviewed client charts. Maintained inventory control and balanced daily transactions.

- Set service and promotional goals to motivate staff and encourage teamwork.
- Increased food and product sales and consistently met or exceeded sales goals.

OTHER WORK EXPERIENCE:

UNIVERSITY HEIGHTS HEALTH CENTER, Albany, NY   1990 to 1993

Licensed Practical Nurse - Provided all aspects of Nursing care.
- Supervised four nurse's aides.
- Consulted with family members and patients to solve problems and address issues.

EDUCATION:

ELMIRA/NURSING SCHOOL, Elmira, NY   1990

Two years education; graduated as Licensed Practical Nurse.

DEBORAH DOOLEY
111 Gordon Road
Westchester, NY 12030
(212) 458-7657

JOB OBJECTIVE

Secretarial position in an office using my organizational skills and ability to perform a wide variety of duties.

SECRETARIAL SKILLS

Notary Public	Macintosh Computer: *Excel, Write Now, Filemaker, QuarkXPress*		
Payroll	Bookkeeping	Accounting Reports	Purchasing
Public Relations	Telephone Skills	Team Player	Trustworthy & Reliable

WORK HISTORY

Swan House, Estate of Gloria Vanderbilt, Westchester, NY
Estate Secretary   **1992 to present**

Perform secretarial function for the operation of the estate. Report to Manager of Estate, Accounting Manager, and Ms. Vanderbilt.

- Process payroll for permanent staff of 11; summer staff of over 20.
- Prepare quarterly Federal and State Payroll Tax statements and annual W-2 forms.
- Verify, process, and record billings for estate and personal accounts.
- Reconcile checking accounts and bank statements.
- Order office supplies and personal items; maintain detailed records on orders; follow-up and verify order delivery and correctness.
- Maintain file of charitable contributions; sort and verify each; prepare annual statement for accountant.
- Prepare monthly accounting reports for other business units.
- Assist with complicated social event planning and follow through.

The Travel Shop, Scarsdale, NY
Intern   **1991**

Part-time two month internship for full service travel agency during college.

- Performed secretarial duties—ordered supplies and catalogs; screened phone calls; ran errands.
- Assisted in setting up new office.

EDUCATION

Long Island Community College, New Rochelle, NY   **1990**
AAS - Travel and Tourism

ELISSA M. CLARK
6906 Foxboro Lane
Bloomfield, IN 46327
(317) 758-5618

CAREER SUMMARY

Three years of experience in information systems, marketing, and advertising. Areas of expertise include excellent communication skills, supervisory ability, and superb computer skills (mainframe, network, and PC arenas).

PROFESSIONAL EXPERIENCE

NORTH AMERICA TIRE, Midland, IN, 1995–Present

Programmer Analyst
Primary responsibility involves creating and maintaining DB2 tables on a daily basis for the United States and Canada. Utilize COBOL II in a TSO environment to generate customer and product sales reports weekly for management staff. Program with FOCUS or BMC to provide ad hoc reports involving part numbers, tread design, sales figures, etc. On call to monitor program performance for nightly batch runs. Assist Human Resources with college recruiting.

- Completed five major projects, all of which were highly visible involving Export Sales, Commercial IS Budget System, Returned Goods, MAST SFA, and Michelin Tire Fill-Rate.
- Participated in accelerated System Engineering Development Program designed to quickly raise programming skills to an experienced level.
- Serve as a Social Coordinator for the Sales Information and Logistics teams.

STATE OF ALABAMA, Disability Adjudication Section, Shelby, AL, 1994

Information Systems Intern
Composed a *Quick-n-Easy Guide to Learning Lotus.* Provided multiple spreadsheets in Lotus. Trained approximately 10 human resource staff with Lotus 1-2-3, WordPerfect, Windows, and basic computer skills when appropriate.

MASONS CLEANERS, Conners, AL, 1993–1995

Advertising Assistant (part-time)
Assisted with general office duties as well as public relations writing and newspaper advertising for a chain of three stores involving 25 employees.

- Responsible for arranging a marketing analysis for several business clients and for the implementation of marketing programs to ensure the highest possible gain.
- Headed the 1993 summer marketing campaign.

EDUCATION

The University of Georgia, Athens, GA
  Bachelor of Business Administration, Major in Management Information Systems;
  Excelled in English/writing courses, 4.0; Dean's List.

COMPUTER SKILLS

  COBOL II, FOCUS, PASCAL, Visual Basic, DB2, SQL, BMC, JCL, TPX, TSO, ZEKE, LAN/WAN, Microsoft Office, Lotus 1-2-3, WordPerfect, DOS 6.2, OS/2, Windows, Windows NT.

ACTIVITIES

  Society of Management Information Systems
  Leadership Counsel in Campus Fellowship—Social Director
  Alpha Delta Pi Sorority

SALLY J. CURTIN
13623 Samantha Drive
Silver Heights, MI 49212
(810) 222-2955

CAREER SUMMARY

Versatile, knowledgeable, detail-oriented program coordinator with over four years' experience in lightweight racing bicycle pre-production vehicle build and vehicle test programs. Excellent oral and written communication skills, as well as administrative and organizational abilities. Extensive experience with computer applications.

EMPLOYMENT HISTORY

MANPOWER, Lansing, MI

<u>Program Coordinator</u>, 1994–Present

Contracted to Track Bicycle Manufacturing Engineering Division.

Responsible for determining the magnitude of future mule, alpha, beta, prototype, and pilot build programs. Issue Build Authorization Documents used to release and order parts for build program. Conduct meetings with management, engineering, financial, and scheduling departments. Manage builds within Track Bike Assembly: body, paint, trim, and chassis. Interface with union representatives. Establish ongoing communication with marketing division to schedule and prepare bicycles for various shows.

- Promoted from assistant coordinator.
- Trained two peers as program coordinators with outstanding results.
- Recommended and instituted new procedures.
- Improved time and cost considerations within life cycle of program.
- Routinely performed work outside job description.
- Helped save approximately 25% of shipping costs.
- Commended by upper management for continuous improvement and recommending new ideas.
- Designed systems to improve customer service and satisfaction.
- Created program approval form which greatly reduced waste.

RESOURCES UNLIMITED, Lansing, MI

<u>Program Specialist</u>, 1991–1993

Contracted to Swift Bicycles, Reliability & Test Division.

Assisted in preparation of future bicycles test programs, shows, and engineering rides. Ensured correct parts were installed. Arranged durability reviews and inspections. Maintained test fleet. Assisted with preparation of program and durability reports. Tracked bicycles through the Part Tracking System.

SPECIAL SKILLS

Utilized Compaq 4/661 and Apple Macintosh II hardware systems and the following software programs: Microsoft Word, Excel, PowerPoint, Lotus Notes, EDSNET, AEC Info Manager, Calendar Maker and MacDraw II.

EDUCATION

Davenport College of Business, Grand Rapids, MI
1988 Graduate
<u>Bachelor of Business Administration</u>
Major: General Business
Minors: Communication, Mathematics, and Social Science

18 Rust Street   Ballwin, NY 12658   518-739-4310

OBJECTIVE: **Writing or Publishing**

SUMMARY: Disciplined, imaginative, and talented writer who works in a variety of genre. Hardworking, dependable, and creative leader. Able to learn on the job and fulfill many roles. Team player with demonstrated ability to establish excellent working relationships with both co-workers and management.

WORK EXPERIENCE: *Substitute Teacher*   *1997 to present*
SCHUYLERVILLE CENTRAL SCHOOL DISTRICT, Schuylerville, NY
Fill in for regular teachers as needed—follow lesson plans, establish classroom control and discipline, complete daily routine.

Student Teacher   *1997*
SCHUYLERVILLE CENTRAL SCHOOL DISTRICT

Waitress (15 to 40 hours/week)   *1995 to present*
THE INN at BALLWIN, Ballwin, NY
Provide professional, courteous service to patrons of 38-room inn with 45-seat dining room. Set up tables and complete kitchen prep prior to opening. Greet customers, suggest specials, take orders, and serve meals. Close register and perform nightly bookkeeping. Fill in as necessary for receptionist, hostess, and bus staff.

- Train new employees on computer and order fulfillment.
- Proactively cross sell—relate history of inn, show rooms, describe range of services.
- Co-create staff schedule.

INTERESTS: Creative writing—stories, poems, essays
Journalism—feature stories, columns

EDUCATION: Bachelor of Science, Elementary Education; Concentration: English
COLLEGE OF ST. ROSE, Albany, NY   1998

Associate of Arts & Sciences - Business Administration
SCHENECTADY COUNTY COMMUNITY COLLEGE,
Schenectady, NY   1994

JERZY KRAWCZYK
450 Reed Drive
Newark, DE 19702
(302) 555-1466

CAREER SUMMARY

Extensive experience with machine set-up, operation, and repair involving industrial presses (75 ton–600 ton) within a manufacturing environment. Acquired specific skill sets associated with the manufacturing of compressors, pumps and turbines. Areas of expertise include staff supervision and training, quality control, and ability to follow detailed blueprints. Described by supervisor and management as being loyal, dedicated, flexible, and positive.

EMPLOYMENT HISTORY

TRIAD COMPANY, Trenton, NJ   1990–Present
Set-up Operator (Newcoor Press)

- Employed with one of the area's largest manufacturers of heating and air conditioning units for residential use.
- Began as an entry level Spot Welder. Advanced to Manual Punch Press Operator (75 ton–600 ton). Promoted to Set-up and Die Changeover before being advanced to Newcoor Set-up Operator.
- Responsible for the operation of a $3.5 million multi-functional Newcoor Press that supplied three different assembly lines with just-in-time (JIT) production affecting over 600 line employees.
- Served as Area Team Coordinator for the recent implementation of a state-of-the-art Demand Flow Technology System (DFT) responsible for reducing inventory, improving quality and safety, and promoting more efficient team work.
- Acted as Team Leader over six employees (four Press Operators and two Lift Truck Operators).
- Read blueprints to ensure proper specifications for each set-up. Involved with up to 50 changeovers per day using sophisticated electronic equipment and systems.
- Trained new and existing staff on all three shifts involving set-up, maintenance procedures, machine operation, and quality control.
- Attended weekly Safety Committee meetings working on quality and safety issues.

TRANSLIFT, INC., Trenton, NJ   1983–1989
Inspector

- Employed with one of the country's largest manufacturers of compressors, pumps, and turbines used by the United States Navy and foreign countries.
- Began as entry level Lift Truck Operator. Advanced to Shipping and Receiving Clerk then to Testing Technician before becoming an Inspector.
- Responsible for final inspection of all finished parts prior to shipment.
- Labeled and monitored all scrap and defective parts.

EDUCATION

Fundamental Vocational School, Zakrzowek, Poland
Graduate with specialty in operation of heavy manufacturing equipment.

Triad Company, Trenton, NJ
Classes in Quality Control, Blueprints, New Equipment Training, Basic Die and Press Set-up, Safety, and Cultural Diversity

CAMILLA A. JOHNSON

332 Fox Grove Place   (H) (908) 332-1234
Summit, NJ 08873   (W) (908) 774-4434

EDUCATION

<u>University of Minnesota</u>, St. Paul, MN, 1997
> Ph.D., Materials Science and Engineering, GPA 7.8 / 8.0
> Thesis: Micromechanisms of Deformation in Crosslinkable Oriented Polymers

<u>University of Virginia</u>, Charlottesville, VA, 1990
> Master of Science, Materials Science, GPA 3.7 / 4.0
> Thesis: Synthesis of Aluminum-Lithium Alloys with High Lithium Content

<u>National Institute of Applied Sciences</u>, Lyon, France, 1988
> Diploma of "Engineer I.N.S.A.," Material Physics Engineering
> Thesis: Rubber Reinforced Epoxy Resin

EXPERIENCE

UNIVERSITY OF MINNESOTA, Dept. of Materials Science and Engineering, St. Paul, MN
<u>Graduate Research Assistant</u>   1994–1997

- Investigated newly designed aramid fibers as part of a team of organic chemists and materials scientists.
- Determined the relationship between deformation behavior and microstructural characteristics.
- Specified potential microstructures for the next generation of polymer fibers.
- Teaching assistant for "Applied Polymer Processing" class (MSE 414), Fall 1996.
- Ultramicrotomy laboratory instructor for "Polymer Microscopy Short Course: UM Engineering Conference for Professionals," June 1996.
- Technical skills developed include:

  > *Mechanical testing*—developed test to transversely compress eight-micron fibers by adapting an interfacial test machine at Oak Ridge National Laboratories.
  > *X-ray diffraction*—identified structure of PPTA-co-XTA copolymer fibers.
  > *Molecular modeling and image simulations*—using Polygraf and CERIUS software packages.
  > *Low voltage SEM, TEM and low dose HREM of polymers*—see HREM on cover of Materials Research Society Bulletin, 20(9), September 1997.

ALLEN CHEMICAL, Minneapolis, MN
<u>Contract Engineer</u>   1993–1994
> Investigated continuous-fiber ceramic composites. Research included optimization of processing conditions (silicon nitride powder processing, tape casting, hot pressing, etc.) and product analysis.

UNIVERSITY OF VIRGINIA, Dept. of Materials Science, Charlottesville, VA
<u>Graduate Research Assistant</u>   1988–1990
> Related mechanical properties and corrosion resistance to the microstructure of new rapidly solidified A1-Li-Mg alloys. Specified alloys for further study.

ARTHUR S. KAHKONEN
3216 HALLOWEEN DRIVE
FARMINGTON HILLS, MI 48503
(810) 209-4325

Offering 10 years of experience in a broad range of business areas, including finance, leasing, accounting, lease administration, credit underwriting, marketing, and human resources. Experienced in financial analysis, risk assessment, and budget management. Knowledgeable in IBM/compatibles, DOS, and Apple PCs. Proficient in Excel, Word for Windows, PageMaker, and HP 17B Financial Calculator. Strong problem-solving and analytical skills. Effective interpersonal and group communication skills. Dedication to high quality standards and continuous process improvement.

EXPERIENCE AND ACCOMPLISHMENTS

Financial and Credit Operations

- Managed risk and profitability for $40 million lease portfolio.
- Reevaluated credit guidelines and developed upgraded credit scoring system, reducing annual budget by $75K.
- Consolidated 10+ order and service contracts into two streamlined forms, simplifying paperwork for sales force and eliminating redundancies. Resulted in annual savings of $75K.
- Negotiated and structured lease proposals, contract terms, and conditions.
- Performed general accounting functions—journals and reconciliations, general ledger, accounts receivable, accounts payable, and budget forecasting. Managed and reconciled inter-company accounts.

Management and Administration

- Managed and directed staff of 17 in the daily operations of financial and credit operations, central order and lease administration, and lease marketing for a national manufacturer of shipping and mailing equipment. Managed a $700K annual departmental budget.
- Reduced budget expenses by $20K through consolidation of staff functions.
- Reviewed all processes and procedures from initial order to shipping of product. Recommended changes resulting in reduction of average order turn-around time from 10–15 days to five days.

Sales and Marketing

- Marketed lease programs to clients, sales branches, and dealers.
- Assisted in the development of special marketing promotions and programs.
- Operated own business selling educational software and toys. Planned and conducted sales events, fundraisers, and product demonstrations. Called on key clients to present marketing promotions and build relationships.
- Developed Maturing Lease Program to track near-future lease expirations and remarketing of used equipment.

Human Resources/Training & Development

- Recruited, interviewed, and selected department and field employees.
- Designed, developed, and conducted training on lease marketing for population of 800+ sales and staff personnel.
- Established job objectives and conducted performance reviews for all direct reports.
- Served on Training Committee to train employees in customer service, quality, and other professional programs.

EMPLOYMENT HISTORY

Educational Consultant, part-time	Self-employed, Wilmington, NC	1996–Present
Financial Services Manager	First Northern Leasing, Hayward, CA	1991–1995
Credit Analyst	Barondata Corporation, San Leandro, CA	1988–1990

EDUCATION

Associate of Science, Computer Data Processing, Massachusetts Bay College, Wellesley, MA, 1989
Seminars on **Creative Leasing, Lease Marketing, Advanced Structuring & Lease Analysis**, and **Credit Risk Assessment**, Ammembal, Halladay & Isom Lease Education, Salt Lake City, UT, 1990–1995
Certificate in Financial Credit Management, National Association of Credit Management, Lexington, MA, 1988

ESPERANZA R. DIAZ
(518) 584-8820

91 Dorothy Street
Saratoga Springs, NY 12866

SUMMARY: Non-judgmental, committed, and caring. Good listener who relates well with people. Team player. Interested in women's health issues.

EDUCATION: **Skidmore College,** Saratoga Springs, NY

Bachelor of Science in Social Work   1997
     Cum laude; Departmental Honors

RELEVANT COURSEWORK:

Social Psychology	Women's Bodies and Minds
Social Work Practice I and II	Values and Interpersonal Skills
Behavior and Social Environment	

INTERNSHIP: **Planned Parenthood Health Services of Northeastern New York, Inc.,**
Schenectady, NY   January–May, 1997
Counseling Intern (Glens Falls, NY site)

Full-time (35 hour/week) internship in full-service clinic providing health care and reproductive services to general public clientele without regard to personal financial resources.

- Provide office and phone counseling on reproductive health.
- Conduct pregnancy tests and urinalysis.
- Interview, counsel, and perform work-up for abortions.
- Counsel and educate clients on contraceptive/reproductive information; facilitate decision-making.
- Document client information in charts and log book.
- Participate as Team Member for site.
- Present Universal HIV Education to patients.

WORK HISTORY:

Pine Manor Tennis Camp, Chestnut Hill, MA   Summers, 1992–1996
Girls' Head Counselor (1993, 1994)
Counselor/Instructor (1990–1992)

Full-time summer job at tennis day camp for youth ages 7 to 16.

- Instructor/Counselor for 8 campers of varied ages for full-day program.
- Planned and conducted instructional and recreational program daily.
- Developed and administered discipline and reward system to deal with behavioral problems.

Ronald Marcus, M.D., Brookline, MA   1993–1995
Office Clerk

- Answered phones, made appointments, filed paperwork and charts.

VOLUNTEER & EXTRACURRICULAR ACTIVITIES:

Skidmore Tennis Team	1993–1997
Boston Area Thanksgiving Dinner for People with AIDS	1993–1997
Skidmore AIDS Project	1997

LISA C. CERUTTI

P.O. Box 606 Highland Parkway   518-969-5992 (Home)
Lake Louise, NY 12486   518-334-1005 (Work)

SUMMARY:

Goal-oriented, highly organized, and skilled at successfully managing multiple tasks. Excellent public speaking, writing, and public relations skills. Demonstrated ability to effectively coordinate public and private sector projects and partnerships. Skilled in IBM-PC; Lotus 1-2-3, Word for Windows, Microsoft Works, WordPerfect, PageMaker, FoxPro, NetScape, and Pegasus; experience in using the Internet.

PROFESSIONAL EXPERIENCE:

Research Associate/Liaison, Center for Technology in Government
New York State Forum for Information Resource Management   Feb. 1997 to present
Public/private partnership which serves to coordinate, streamline, and integrate technological solutions to agency and department operations, problems and opportunities throughout New York State government.

- Serve on operations team to demonstrate and promote prototypes; assist project coordinator and technical team in planning public relations strategies; write press releases and newsletter articles. Projects include: Geographic Information System Cooperative Project, Internet Kickoff Workshop, and Office of Mental Health Psychiatric Assessment.
- Conduct research and write 'White Papers' at request of NYS Administration, for example, "Data Center Consolidation."
- Represent Center for Technology in Government at Government Technology Conference.
- Assist in managing Forum Computer Bulletin Board System.
- Member, Standing Committee of the Center for Technology in Government.

Graduate Assistant, Public Administration Dept., State University of New York   Sept. 1997 to present
- Administrative Assistant in graduate school office.

EDUCATION:

Master of Public Administration, Concentration in Public Management   1998
Nelson A. Rockefeller College of Public Affairs & Policy, State University of New York at Albany

Bachelor of Science—Liberal Studies, Concentration in Psychology and Sociology   January 1996
Regents College University of the State of New York, State University of New York at Albany

Associate in Applied Science—Broadcast Communications   May 1993
Adirondack Community College, Queensbury, NY

HONORS:

Phi Theta Kappa • Adirondack Broadcast Association, ACC President's Cup Award for Academic Excellence, 1992 • JayCees Outstanding Young New Yorker Contest, 1st place, County, District, Regional; 2nd place, State • American Legion Oratorical Contest, 1st place, Local, County, District; 2nd place, Zone

VOLUNTEER ACTIVITIES:

Member, *Student Association—Graduate School of Public Administration & Public Policy*
Treasurer, Fall 1997–Spring 1998
- Prepare budget application for approval by the Graduate Student Association.
- Plan and execute fundraising activities.

Member, *Adirondack Girl Scouts*   1980 to present
Officer and Board Member, 1987–1988

MARNY LANDS
1456 Vista Court
Valencia, CA 93460
(248) 860-9987
Mlands@coastnet.net

HIGHLIGHTS OF QUALIFICATIONS

- A hardworking achiever who has earned additional job functions, responsibilities and promotions based upon performance.
- A self-motivated and creative individual with strong interpersonal skills.
- Works well under pressure by skillfully setting priorities and managing multiple tasks.
- Effectively analyzes and satisfies client needs.
- Makes oral presentations to management of major corporations such as Anheuser Busch, Blue Cross, Textron and Litton Industries with positive sales results.

MANAGEMENT AND CLIENT RELATIONS

- Developed excellent client relationship skills by successfully managing difficult clients and sensitive correspondence issues.
- Coordinated sales programs including catered events, outings, seasonal consignment tickets, VIP cards and private parties.
- Trained new sales representatives by discussing sales strategies and techniques, procedures and client accounts.
- Built solid relationships with clients through honesty, reliability and timely follow through.

MARKETING AND SALES

- Sold the largest catered event in Six Flags California history with 16,000 in attendance and $435,000 in revenue.
- Increased annual catered event sales in territory 53%, raising territory revenue to over $2 million.
- Achieved sales success through effective target market identification, skillful oral and written presentations, and creative event planning and organization.
- Designed letters and promotional materials that helped increase sales.
- Promoted to Corporate Sales Representative, responsible for the largest revenue grossing territory in California.

EMPLOYMENT HISTORY

Corporate Sales Representative, Six Flags California, Valencia, CA 1996–present
Senior Sales Representative, MobileComm-Bell South, Torrance, CA 1995
Senior Phone Representative, Health Network Insurance, Redland, CA 1993–1995

EDUCATION

BACHELOR OF ARTS IN SPEECH COMMUNICATION, California State University Northridge 1994
Course Highlights: Communication • Journalism • Radio/TV/Film • Windows 95 proficient.

AWARDS AND AFFILIATIONS

- Awarded top Corporate Sales Representative for Six Flags California in 1997.
- Member of AIRC, a networking association for area corporations.
- Raised money annually for the American Heart Association at California State University Northridge.
- Served as chairman for the Newsletter, Big Brother and Rush committees for Alpha Phi Sorority.
- Participated in university-wide fund raising events for Los Angeles Children's Hospital and delivered toys to hospitalized children.

ROBERTA FREEDMAN

43 Rider Road • Queensmount, NY 12385

(518) 928-1748 • rfreedman@nynet.com

SUMMARY: Fluent in Russian language—speaking, listening, writing, and reading. Reading fluency in German. Recent living and work experience in Moscow and thorough knowledge of Russian history, literature, culture and customs. Demonstrated ability to learn quickly, adapt to unexpected and new situations, and negotiate successfully. Proficient in Macintosh and Microsoft Word; familiar with IBM-PC.

INTERNATIONAL
EXPERIENCE: *Financial and Business News,* Moscow, Russia   2/98 to 4/98

Style Editor and Translator - Translated and edited Russian language business articles to English for Western edition of monthly business publication with worldwide distribution. Reported to Chief Editor.

Lingua Rex School, Moscow, Russia   2/98 to 5/98

English Teacher - Taught English language to grades 7 to 9; incorporated history, literature, and music into lessons.

Private English Tutor, Moscow, Russia   2/98 to 5/98

Tutored private family in English language.

EDUCATION: *Connecticut College,* New London, CT   12/97

Bachelor of Arts - Russian & Eastern European Studies
3.5 GPA in major; 3.1 GPA overall; earned 50% of total college expenses through part-time campus jobs and Army Reserve.

U. S. Army Defense Language Institute, Monterey, CA   4/96
Graduate - Russian Basic Course; Defense Language Proficiency Level III
Completed 12 month course in 8 months.
Association of the U.S. Army Achievement Award for GPA and Test Scores.

MILITARY
EXPERIENCE: *U. S. Army Reserve,* Ft. Devens, MA   2/93 to 2/98
Russian Linguist, Rank of Specialist

VOLUNTEER
EXPERIENCE: *Tutoring Plus,* Cambridge, MA   9/95 to 12/97
Tutor - English, math, reading, and writing for disadvantaged children.

MARY A. LEONARD

8754 N. Cottage Drive
Baton Rouge, LA 71118
(513) 976-2345

HIGHLIGHTS OF QUALIFICATIONS

Quality-conscious, professional employment consultant with outstanding organizational skills. Enthusiastic, dedicated, efficient coordinator of temporary staff employees and incoming job orders. Energetic, dependable team player with proven track record of placements and satisfied customers.

EMPLOYMENT HISTORY

Johnson Temporary Employment, Inc., Baton Rouge, LA

EMPLOYMENT CONSULTANT   *1997–CURRENT*

Interview and evaluate prospective temporary personnel. Test employment skills and define employment needs. Match best qualified personnel to meet clients' employment needs. Conduct follow-up with companies to ensure satisfaction and evaluate future business opportunities. Negotiate billing rates, ensuring positive working relationship with clientele.

- Integral part of overall team effort, resulting in increase in billing hours of over one-third.
- Proficient in time management, thereby increasing efficiency.
- Evaluate employees weekly on PC: Windows, WordPerfect, Excel and Lotus 1-2-3.
- Interface with customer base of 70 clients on a monthly basis.
- Improve customer service by filling 20+ orders per week, doubling original capability.
- Manage, direct, and assign up to 30 temporary employees at a given time.
- Responsible for training new consultants.

Western Life Insurance Company, Shreveport, LA

ADMINISTRATIVE ASSISTANT   *1996*

Processed applications and forwarded to home office. Monitored policies during underwriting process. Prepared information for special presentations. Typed letters, proposals and memoranda. Coordinated travel arrangements with meeting locations. Maintained excellent PC skills.

Des Moines Educational Association, Des Moines, IA

ADMINISTRATIVE ASSISTANT/EXECUTIVE SECRETARY   *1993–1995*

Processed contribution checks from receipt to deposit. Informed management of balances of accounts for investment purposes. Entered transactions into corporate records. Generated daily, monthly, and annual reports. Monitored contributors and sent monthly reminders. Updated and expanded database of 3,000+ files. Edited prepared letters, proposals, and memoranda for president. Informed Board of Directors of contributors on a monthly basis. Maintained inventory of office supplies and equipment.

EDUCATION

American Institute of Business, Des Moines, IA
Associate of Business Degree, May 1989

References Available Upon Request

STEPHANIE PETERSON

333 Walter Drive   **Springdale, NY 12829**   **(518) 593-2857**

EDUCATION:

State University of New York at Plattsburgh   August 1996
Bachelor of Science, Mass Communication; Concentration—TV Production

EXPERIENCE AND SKILLS:

Producer and Director
- *Producer/Director* of "The Beat," a daily half-hour music video show produced for PSTV. (Spring 1993)
- *Producer/Director* of "Beat Best," a weekly one-hour music video countdown show for PSTV. (Spring 1993)
- *Teaching Assistant*—Mass Media 375, "Television Studio Production"—hands-on instruction for upper-level students in all aspects of TV studio operation and production. (Spring 1993)

Talent
- *Host*—"Plattsburgh After Hours" (Fall 1994 to 1996)
- *VJ*—"The Beat" (Fall 1995)

Awarded PSTV Best Talent (Spring 1995)
- *DJ and Owner*—Magical Notes DJ service. Engagements include weddings, dances, banquets, and Bar Mitzvahs. (Oct. 1991 to present)

Technical Skills
- *Studio Technician*—All aspects of in-house TV production and occasional commercial field shooting for Capital District station. (Sept. 1996 to present)
- *Videographer and Tape Editor* — "The Three-Umpire System," a technical training video produced on location for the New York State Association of Softball Umpires. (Fall 1995)
- *Crew Chief, Director, Technical Director, Assistant Director, Audio Engineer, Lighting Engineer, Character Generator Operator, Master Control Operator, Videographer, TelePrompter Operator, Videotape Editor*—PSTV—Cable Channel 10. (1994 to 1996)

Internship
- *Television Production Intern,* WTEN Ch. 10, ABC affiliate in Albany, NY. (May to Aug. 1996)

WORK HISTORY:

WTEN Channel 10, **Studio technician.** (Sept. 1996 to present)
Plattsburgh Motor Service, **Counter person**—Saturdays. (Oct. 1995 to May 1996)
PSTV Equipment Room, **Attendant**—work-study. (Sept. 1994 to May 1995)
WKAJ-AM 900 Radio, **Board operator.** (Apr. 1992 to July 1992)

EXTRACURRICULAR ACTIVITIES:

SUNY–Plattsburgh Forensics Team (Fall 1992 to Spring 1994)
    Tournament Awards: 2nd–Improvisation Pairs (SUNY–Binghampton); 5th–Dramatic Duo, After-Dinner Speaking (SUNY–Plattsburgh); 5th–Improvisation Pairs (Southern Connecticut)
Chemistry Van Project (Public School Outreach Program)—Magician (Spring 1994 to Spring 1996)
Alpha Epsilon Rho/National Broadcast Society—Member (1994 to present)

ANN REGAN-MURPHY

3215 Lorrimar Road

Long Island, NY 14072

(716) 546-2950

CAREER SUMMARY

Eight years' experience in the field of education, emphasizing the college application process. Skilled with financial/scholarship search on individual and group counseling.

PROFESSIONAL EXPERIENCE

CENTRALIA HIGH SCHOOL, Rhinebeck, New York   1990–1998
Administrative Assistant for Guidance Services

Coordinated college application process. Responsible for completion of transcripts, letters of recommendation, student activity sheets, and supplemental application information. Coordinated all guidance office, college, career, and military resources and services. Responsible for coordinating library materials, files, videos, and the Discover software package. Disseminated college entrance exam information, financial aid, and scholarship information. Scheduled college visitation, open house, and college fairs. Provided support to students with reference to academic and personal issues. Advised former students regarding advanced educational opportunities.

- Developed/implemented and co-taught required College 101 curriculum.
- Served as guidance liaison to faculty, students, parents, principal's office, district office, elementary and middle schools, and community groups.
- Coordinated and prioritized student, parent, faculty, administrative support staff, and committee meetings for guidance counselors.
- Assisted with implementation, coordination, and monitoring of peer counseling and tutoring programs.
- Worked with development of guidance budget and master schedule.
- Computerized, generated, and updated student records.
- Published guidance information newsletter periodically.
- Handled the Computerized Information Math System (CIMS) for first through sixth grade.

OTHER EMPLOYMENT POSITIONS

Statistical Secretary for University of Kansas—Board of Educational Research

Business Assistant (A/P, A/R) for Mercedes/Benz dealership

Inventory/Sales Secretary for Cadillac dealership

EDUCATION AND TRAINING

Mohawk Valley Community College, Utica, New York
Associate in Applied Science (Secretarial Science)—Dean's List

Board of Cooperative Education Services (BOCES)
Computer Program Scheduling Workshop
Computerized Information Math System Training

RALPH L. SMITH
2436 Rue Mandoline Street
Mandeville, LA 70230
(504) 230-5287

CAREER SUMMARY

Approximately 15 years' experience in product manufacturing and the automotive technician field. Areas of expertise include electrical, electronic, and mechanical analysis and diagnosis of faulty vehicles and production-related equipment. Familiar with the repair of pneumatic and hydraulic processes. Ability to read blueprints and hydraulic and electrical schematics and perform computer diagnostic tests.

PROFESSIONAL EXPERIENCE

NELSON FORD, INCORPORATED, Biloxi, LA   1995–1998
Automotive Technician

Responsible for diagnosis and repair of new and used automobiles. Certified by Ford Motor Company and received the Automotive Service of Excellence in Heating and Air Conditioning and Electrical and Electronic Diagnosis. Skilled in Driveability Computer Electronic Diagnosis.

AMERICAN AMBULANCE, Shreveport, LA   1992–1994
Automotive Technician

Provided service and repairs on ambulances and specially-equipped vans for the physically handicapped. Installed hand controls, electric lifts, and floors.

SHREVEPORT OLDSMOBILE/PONTIAC, Shreveport, LA   1988–1992
Automotive Technician

Certified by General Motors in the areas of Automotive Electrical and Electronic Repair, Driveability Computer Diagnosis, Heating and Air Conditioning and Transmission Repair.

AT&T CONSUMER PRODUCTS MANUFACTURING PLANT, Shreveport, LA   1983–1987
Material Handler/Electrical Repair

Conducted all electrical and mechanical repairs of conveyor lines and equipment associated with the production of telephones. Worked with oscilloscopes and digital multimeters. Distributed and maintained adequate inventory levels for production. Trained in hazardous waste handling.

EDUCATION/TRAINING AND COMMUNITY INVOLVEMENT

Woodlawn High School, Shreveport, LA
Graduate

Ford Motor Company
Electronic Systems, Automotive Electronics, and Electronic Engine Control

General Motors Corporation
Climate Control, ASE Refrigerant Recovery and Recycling Review Program, Transmissions: Automatic and Manual, Specialized Electronic Training and numerous other specialized classes

Community Involvement
Involved in local community organizations, including the Masonic Lodge, Muscular Dystrophy Association (as well as the MDA Labor Day Telethon) and the Easter Seal campaign.

KEVIN HORTON
217 Christmas Court • Springdale, NY 12345 • 518-306-1846

SUMMARY

Self-directed and motivated with record of success in sales and customer service. Learn quickly and adapt well to change. Work effectively with clients, co-workers, and employees.

WORK HISTORY

COLDBANK ROOHAN REALTY — Springdale, NY

Sales Associate — **Jan. 1996 to present**

Residential real estate sales requiring knowledge of legal aspects of property transactions, local and regional market information, and mortgage rates and options.

- Perform Competitive Market Analysis (CMA) for prospective sellers.
- Determine effective marketing strategies for properties including initial selling price, repairs and improvements, advertisements, listing information, and open house dates.
- Work closely with seller to adjust strategies for current market.

KEVIN HORTON PAINTING — Springdale, NY

Owner — **May 1993 to Dec. 1995**

Interior and exterior residential painting and staining. Supervised crew of up to three employees.

- Solicited customers, prepared estimates, hired and scheduled crew, obtained necessary materials and equipment, resolved customer questions and problems, performed bookkeeping.
- Expanded business through referrals from satisfied customers.

RICHARD HORTON PAINTING — Springdale, NY

Job Site Supervisor — **1992 to 1993**

Managed and directed daily activities of three employees.

Painter — **Summers 1987 to 1993**

EDUCATION

HARTWICK COLLEGE — Oneonta, NY
- Bachelor of Arts - Economics — May 1994

SPRINGDALE HIGH SCHOOL — Springdale, NY
- Regents Diploma — 1990
- Key Club Award - Athlete of the Year — 1990

TRAINING

Coldbank Fast Start — 1995

NYS Real Estate Licensing Course — 1995

ACTIVITIES & INTERESTS

Alpha Chi Rho Fraternity — 1992–1994
Hartwick Men's Basketball Team — 1990–1993
High School Summer Basketball League Coach — 1990, 1992, 1994
Active in Skiing, Basketball, and Softball — Current

THERESA P. MINOT

962 Voltaire Lane
Tempe, AZ 85283
602-785-8370
tminot@evernet.net

CAPABILITY SUMMARY:

- Efficient and organized; able to meet deadlines
- Conscientious and quality conscious
- Professional attitude with ability to work with people at all levels
- Fast learner who takes initiative
- Maintain composure in high-pressure situations

OFFICE SKILLS

Secretarial

- Typing 60 wpm, shorthand, transcription
- Operate IBM and Macintosh computers
- Familiar with WordPerfect, Scriptset, and Lotus 1-2-3
- Schedule appointments and make travel arrangements
- Organize and maintain files
- Compose and type routine correspondence
- Prepare financial and other reports
- Act as receptionist and telephone operator

Accounting

- Enter data to general ledger and balance on daily, weekly, monthly, and yearly basis
- Maintain collateral values on stocks, bonds, and savings passbooks on quarterly basis
- Process and calculate renewal loans
- Process payroll

Supervisory

- Hire and train new personnel
- Supervise up to 10 employees
- Order and maintain office supply and restaurant inventory

WORK HISTORY

Day Care Provider, Mesa, AZ	**1996 to Present**
Minot's Beverage - Payroll Clerk, Tempe, AZ	**1994 to 1996**
Catalina Trust - Secretary, Tucson, AZ	**1989 to 1994**

EDUCATION

Tucson Business College, Tucson, AZ	1989
A.A.S. - Executive Secretarial	

ROBERT C. HARRIMORE

4300 Greenleaf West

Colleyville, MI 48034

(810) 652-1212

CAREER SUMMARY

Over 12 years of experience in sales and retail management. Areas of expertise include excellent public relations, management skills, proven leadership, and supervision of staff.

EMPLOYMENT HISTORY

MICHIGAN STAIRS AND MILL INC., Niles Township, MI, *1995–1998*

Sales Representative

Dealt with contractors, builders, field superintendents, and homeowners involved with the sale of staircases in new and existing homes. Informed, educated, and assisted builders and direct homeowners regarding styles, material choices, and available options. These options involved interior molding, stringers, hand rails, balusters, newel posts, and caps. Provided quotes, ordered all materials and parts. Scheduled and followed up on all phases of installation.

- Exceptional ability to provide attractive quotes for customers while providing the company with an excellent profit margin.
- Kept three work crews busy most of the year with increasing levels of new business.
- Involved annually with the Builders' Show.

MAIN RIVER GOLF COURSE, Salt River, MI, *1993–1995*

Manager

Responsible for all pro shop staff (15 members), including Starters, Rangers, Cart Staff and Bartenders. Scheduled tee times daily, weekly, and for special events. Organized and sold special golf packages involving banquets, bar, golf carts, and dinner. Ordered all liquor.

- Managed operations with revenues ranging from $4,000 to $12,000 daily and special events on weekends up to $20,000.
- Increased reservations by 25%, resulting in a high guarantee rate.
- Initiated and organized winter billiard leagues to utilize idle clubhouse, resulting in increased off-season revenue.

ALLIED WINDOW CORPORATION, Hope, MI, *1990–1992*

Sales Representative

Responsible for showroom and outside sales to both commercial and residential customers. Sold vinyl replacement windows, storm and entry doors, bows, bays, sliders, and double-hung windows.

- Cited as top salesman for March and November 1991.
- Consistently in the top third of monthly sales.

O'HALLORAN'S BAR, Detroit, MI, *1984–1990*

Owner/Operator

Owned and operated a well-known local Irish pub. Responsible for overall management, ordering, pricing, selling merchandise, hiring, and training employees. Organized outside functions to generate additional revenue.

- Popular stop for area celebrities as well as local residents.
- Neighborhood meeting place to view major sporting events.

MILITARY SERVICE

United States Navy (Submarine Service)

JANETTA VORST
9238 Santo Dr. #15
LaCrosse, WI 53719
(608) 555-4522

PROFESSIONAL EXPERIENCE

AS/400 Produce Marketing Specialist, International Business Machines (IBM), Southfield, MI
1/97 to 1/98

- Completed five-month IBM Sales Training Program.
- Assisted in selling AS/400 systems and applications.
- Performed product presentations.
- Prepared AS/400 configurations and proposals.
- Assisted in product announcement events.

Telephone Service Representative, Chesapeake Directory Sales Co. (Bell Atlantic), Greenbelt, MD
2/96 to 9/96

- Sold Bell Atlantic and GTE yellow pages advertising.
- Performed time management and administrative duties.
- Received Sales Representative awards for top performance.
- Disciplined in the Quality Education Systems (QES).

Marketing Intern, Benefits Group, Inc., Chevy Chase, MD
1/95 to 8/95

- Assisted in selling insurance and financial products.
- Prepared presentations for prospective clients.
- Accompanied sales representatives on joint field calls.
- Made appointments for sales representatives.

Sales Representative, Vector Marketing Corporation, Fairfax, VA
5/94 to 12/94

- Performed professional presentations and acquired referrals.
- Served as key person of the Capital Division office.
- Awarded Top Sales Representative in the Capital and Midwest Divisions.
- Member of the Presidential Club.
- Branch Manager Candidate for the 1994 summer campaign.

EDUCATION

Bachelor of General Studies, The University of Michigan, Ann Arbor, MI, 1995
Concentrations in Marketing and International Studies

- Financed 75% of college expenses through grants, scholarships, and employment.

AWARDS

- William Hamby and Libby Beek George Scholarship
- Wharton School of Business 1990 LEAD Program Alumni

LANGUAGES

- Tagalog (Philippines' main language) and French

A Note on Scannable Resumes

Some organizations to which you send your resume will request a "scannable" copy. This means that your resume will be electronically "scanned," or read into, a computer database program. For this type of resume, eliminate all bold-faced type, underlining, and italics from the page, because these features tend to blur in the scanner. Also, choose a "Sans Serif" font—block letters—rather than "Serif" type, the kind with "trails" on the letters. Make sure you use a lot of descriptive nouns related to your job, such as "Accounting, General Ledger, Accounts Receivable," etc. You may use abbreviations, for instance, B.A., to indicate a college degree or other information, but it is also recommended that you spell out the abbreviation. This will make for a redundant, rather plain-looking resume, but the computer will love it. On the following page is an example of a scannable resume.

BASIL E. BOTTOMS
541 RANDOLPH DRIVE
BUFFINGTON, AL 35758
(205) 823-1234
basilbottoms@AZLINK.net

SUMMARY

Dedicated, professional speech-language pathologist with 8 years' experience providing therapy to clients from ages $1\frac{1}{2}$ to 90. Conduct testing and observation to identify communicative impairments in articulation, language, auditory processing, stuttering, voice and hearing. Work with students in classroom and speech room settings classified as learning disabled, mentally handicapped, speech impaired, language impaired, hearing impaired, autistic, Down's syndrome and cleft palate. Develop, implement, and coordinate therapy programs utilizing goal based remediation in individual and group sessions. Provide reassessment and evaluation of student progress. Treated hospital patients with communicative impairments in both in-patient and out-patient settings. Treated medically diagnosed cases of aphasia, dysphagia, apraxia, dysarthria and cerebral palsy. Prepared and maintained initial evaluation reports, daily logs, monthly summary reports, and insurance-related reports.

- Functioned as supervisor for Speech and Hearing Department.
- Chairperson for Planning and Placement Team.
- Reported test results to District Committee, teachers and parents.
- Member of District Committee on Special Education.
- Assigned to School Child Study Team.
- Supervised staff of student teachers.
- Member of Staff Support and MET teams.
- Carried caseload of up to 80 clients.
- Member of School Affairs Committee.

PROFESSIONAL HISTORY

Madison County Schools, Madison, AL	1996–Current
Bay City Schools, Bay City, MS	1994–1996
Clio School System, Clio, MS	1993–1994
McLaren General Hospital, Finch, MS	1992–1993
Fisher-Titus Memorial Hospital, Norwalk, OH	1991–1992
West Hartford School System, West Hartford, CN	1990–1991

EDUCATION

MASTER OF SCIENCE DEGREE, State University College of Buffalo, NY
Teaching Major: Speech-Language Pathology, 1990

BACHELOR OF SCIENCE DEGREE, Ball State University, Muncie, IN
Major: Speech Pathology and Audiology; Minor: Business, 1987
Participated in numerous conventions, seminars, and workshops from 1990 to 1996

PROFESSIONAL MEMBERSHIPS

American Speech-Language-Hearing Association
Speech and Hearing Association of Alabama
Alabama Board of Examiners for Speech Pathology and Audiology

CERTIFICATIONS

State of Mississippi, Department of Education
Provisional Teaching Certificate, Grades K–12 SB

State of Alabama, Department of Education
Professional Certificate, Special Education, N–12
Speech-Language Pathology

SECTION
TWO

CHARTING YOUR COURSE

5

JOB MARKET INFORMATION

In the first section of this workbook, *Preparing for Your Voyage*, you laid the foundation for your job search journey by making life management decisions, documenting your background, skills, and accomplishments, and writing your resume.

In this section, *Charting Your Course*, we will look at directions that you can take to investigate jobs. Information on jobs comes from a variety of sources, and you must plan or chart your course for navigating through these informational waters. You might think of your journey as a voyage where you proceed for a while, then stop at a port to reprovision and plan the next leg. Your job search investigation journey will include researching, exploring the hidden and visible markets, networking, and prospecting.

JOB SEARCH PRINCIPLES

As you chart your course, there are several job search principles to keep in mind.

1. As a successful job seeker, you approach your job search with a positive and optimistic attitude.

2. As a successful job seeker, you know yourself and what you have to offer to a prospective employer.

3. As a successful job seeker, you will access information from a variety of sources including libraries, the Internet, your network, and the local and national media.

4. As a successful job seeker, you plan or chart your course on a regular basis. As in a sailing journey, this course may change based on new information.

You continue to monitor the new information and adjust your course as necessary.

5. As a successful job seeker, you place a high priority on your journey. Do not let anything or anybody take you off your course.

THE VISIBLE JOB MARKET

In order to chart your course, you must take a look at where jobs can be located. There are two major job location categories: the visible job market and the hidden job market. The visible market consists of sources such as want ads, placement offices, recruiting firms, temporary agencies, and professional journal listings. This source of job leads tends to be where all job seekers have an equal chance of obtaining the information.

Want Ads

The want ads, which every job seeker turns to on Sunday in the local paper, represent only a fraction of the positions actually available at any one time. Most estimates say that fewer than 20 percent of actual job openings ever hit the newspaper. Most employers use a variety of recruiting methods to fill available positions; placing a want ad may be used for only certain types of jobs. At any rate, while want ads may be a legitimate source of information about job openings, it should never be the only source because you face the most competition from hundreds of other want ad readers who will respond to the same ads. Spend a few hours on Sunday scanning the entire want ad section, since jobs you may be seeking could be indexed in a variety of ways. Select ads of interest and read each carefully, highlighting the qualifications requested. Then draft a cover letter emphasizing how you meet those qualifications. Mail your cover letter and resume on Tuesday or Wednesday, so your response arrives a day or two later than the crush of letters that are mailed on Sunday or Monday.

A Note on Blind Ads: Blind ads are those which don't list an employer's name or address, just a post office box or newspaper box. If the address is a newspaper box, you will not be able to find the owner. If it is a post office box, though, you can try calling the post office at the ZIP code listed and ask who rents the box. If it is used by a business, the information is public and can be released to you. This information will help you personalize your letter, as well as make a follow-up call possible.

Placement Offices and Professional Journal Listings

Job listings at colleges or other public offices and in professional journal listings should be handled similarly to a want ad response. You should complete a cover letter stating your qualifications in response to those mentioned in the listing. Mail this with your resume, and follow up whenever possible. Keep in mind that these job listings represent less than 10 percent of available jobs, so don't devote too much time and attention to these sources.

Temporary or Contractual Agencies

Temporary or contractual agencies, a visible market source, have become increasingly popular with both employers and job seekers. After the rounds of downsizings that began in the 1970s and have continued into the 1990s, many employers began filling positions through temporary agencies. The growth of this phenomenon is partly due to employers foreseeing a fluctuation in the demand for the work, planning the work as a project with a limited life span, or otherwise not seeing a need for a permanent employee.

More than 20 percent of the work force are not full-time employees. They are independent contractors, temporaries, leased employees, and part-timers. Job assignments for a contracted or temporary employee are by specific task or project rather than by a traditional employer-employee arrangement. Sometimes, this flexible and independent approach has advantages for a job seeker.

Temporary work can allow you to try out new occupations and get inside organizations of interest to you while keeping money coming in and seeking a permanent job. Many employers with a permanent position to fill will employ a temporary to see if the worker performs adequately. This is beneficial to you as well as to the employer because you can see if you like the culture and the type of work you are given. You can keep your name on file with a temporary agency indefinitely and be sent on a variety of assignments throughout the years. Many agencies offer benefits to their employees after a specified period of time. Temporary assignments are available in a wide range of career fields and at many levels of expertise. Some agencies specialize in placing executives and professionals, while others work with office staff or industrial positions. If entering the work force from school, or reentering the work world after many years of unpaid work, temporary work is an excellent way to gain references and experience.

Working with Recruiters

Many job seekers are under the impression that the best and quickest route to a new job is to send their resume to an executive recruiter, then sit back and wait for the interviews. Unfortunately, this approach rarely works that effortlessly. Unlike agents who are motivated to find you work because they will receive a percentage of your pay directly from you, recruiters (or head-hunters) are paid by the employing firm either to present a viable group of candidates for a specific position or to actually bring in the candidate who lands the job. Their compensation, and therefore their interests, lie with the employer, with whom they want to maintain an ongoing relationship in order to be given future assignments.

So how can you, as a job seeker, effectively utilize this system to get your name placed in front of a recruiter who is filling the perfect position for you? There are two basic routes:

1. Write or call a recruiter, describe your background and goals, and ask to be considered for any positions he or she is currently seeking to fill.
2. Ask your network contacts to refer you to appropriate recruiters that they know.

Recruiters are usually working on difficult placement tasks under tight deadlines. They do not have time to spend on unproductive phone calls. However, they are in the relationship business, since most of their candidates come from referrals. If you have been helpful in the past, you might find your recruiter contacts to be helpful to you.

If the recruiter is not currently working on placing someone with your background, he or she might know an internal colleague who would like to talk with you. Also, more recruiting firms are establishing resume databases, which provide them with easily searchable tools to help pull candidates for future searches. Finally, your recruiter contact may be able to give you a lead to an organization that is searching for someone like you, but has decided not to fill the position through a recruiter.

Without such a close relationship to a recruiter, the next best approach is to send a letter to a recruiter who works in your industry or line of expertise. One of the best sources of information on these is *The Directory of Executive Recruiters*, published by Kennedy Publications. It is available in most libraries and bookstores. This directory indexes recruiters by industry, specialty field, and geographic location, and indicates whether they work on retainer or contingency.

Does retainer or contingency make a difference to you? Maybe. The retained firms usually have an exclusive contract to present qualified candidates for a specific position, while the contingency firms may be competing with other recruiters to land the final choice. While neither position is indicative of the quality of the recruiter, there are differences in their approaches. With retained firms, you will be competing with the other candidates in their pool, and the recruiter has no special interest in which of the candidates is hired as long as the pool is strong. Since contingency firms don't get paid unless their candidate is hired, they may get more involved in marketing you. In fact, some contingency firms will try to market you to a wide selection of companies. You need to be sure that your name won't be presented to your current employer or to a company where you already have started a dialogue. You don't want to raise any confusion about who presented your name first, whether it is you or two competing recruiters. Many employers will choose to take you out of consideration rather than get tangled in a dispute about commissions.

Realistically, you can probably expect to generate interest at only 2 to 3 percent of the firms you write. That's not because you are a poor writer or unqualified candidate, but because you have not approached them at a time when they are conducting a search for someone like you. Should you place a follow-up call after sending your letter? Some recruiters will tell you it's a waste of time, while others will say it can help move you along. If you are willing to invest the time in the call and can handle the likely brush-offs you may get from some recruiters, a follow-up call may be advantageous to you.

Your letter to recruiters should include background information, but since your resume will be included, don't be repetitive. Instead, provide more detailed information that's not on your resume, including your salary history and requirements. This is crucial. Also, indicate your career goals and desired location or relocatability. In other words, let the recruiter know your bottom-line desires in order to position yourself properly. Once you are in front of an employer, you and your recruiter must be on the same wavelength in order to preserve both parties' credibility with the employer.

Finally, you can use your networking to put your name in front of appropriate recruiters. Chances are very good that some of your network contacts have established relationships with various recruiters over the years. Your best lead is through a personal referral. So tell your contacts what you are seeking and ask them to refer you to anyone they know who might be able to give you information on opportunities appropriate to you, including referrals to recruiters.

In all your contacts with recruiters, keep some important points in mind. These are professionals whose livelihoods depend on their credibility and integrity.

- Never lie about *anything* in your background. It is too easily discovered.
- Always be professional in your discussions and put your best foot forward.
- Be objective and positive about current or past employers, regardless of how you feel you were treated.
- Follow your recruiter's advice—she knows her corporate clients.
- Don't expect too much—there are many variables that affect your candidacy.

Both contingency and retained recruiters can be an entry into organizations that you might otherwise not be able to penetrate. But to use them effectively, you need to understand their role in the hiring process and work with it. They can be an effective part of your overall strategy; just keep all those other strategies going as well.

The Hidden Job Market

Research has shown that a majority of jobs (60 to 75 percent) are not filled through the visible market, but instead are filled before they become postings or ads. How do they get filled?

They get filled through what the job search practitioners call the "hidden job market." This term simply means filling a position without the use of ads or a recruiting firm. In other words, the organization has an employment need, learns about a qualified job seeker, and fills the position. How has the organization learned about this job seeker? Possibly the job seeker has researched this particular organization and directly contacted the employer just as a job was opening up. Believe it or not, this happens frequently. Or maybe a job seeker previously talked with the hiring manager at a time when nothing was available, but the job seeker followed up on a regular basis until a job became available. Other employers place a great deal of emphasis on recruiting through referrals from current employees. Their reasoning is that a satisfactory, loyal employee will tend to refer the type of people who will fit into the organization and perform well. Other managers will tap into their extended networks of friends and colleagues when they are attempting to fill a particular job and ask for referrals to qualified people looking for that type of position.

With the high cost of newspaper ads and recruiting fees, you can understand why a company would want to fill a job without incurring high costs. So the philosophy here is simple. Don't assume an employer does not need your talents simply because you do not see a want ad in the newspaper or in the other areas of the visible job market. Get in and talk to the manager before the job is advertised. To do this, you can take two major approaches: **networking** and **prospecting.** Because these techniques are so critical to a successful search, we have devoted entire chapters to them.

Briefly, networking is a communication process involving talking to people you know and to people they know and asking them for information, advice, and referrals. Prospecting is a process of identifying companies of interest to you which are likely to have positions that you can fill, and directly approaching the hiring decision maker to set up an appointment to discuss opportunities within that organization. This approach may sound scary to some job seekers, but it can be extremely effective.

So off we go to chart your course. Come with us to learn more about job search research, networking, and prospecting. We will also give you many helpful tips on what to say as you approach potential employers and ideas for your job search correspondence.

FINDING AND USING RESEARCH SOURCES

Throughout your job search, you will be using a variety of research sources to help you find information about jobs, people, employers, and other important topics. You should identify a public library convenient to you that has a good selection of business reference materials. Become familiar with the reference staff, too, because they can help you find hard-to-locate information. Internet sites for specific resources are listed here in parentheses where known. Since sites are added overnight, this list may not be up to date. You can use one of the search engines to look for new sites. These search engines, plus multi-layered sites that contain a diverse collection of resources, are listed at the end of this section.

- For information on subsidiaries and divisions of public and private companies:

    Directory of Corporate Affiliations, National Register Publishing Co.

    America's Corporate Families, Dun & Bradstreet Information Services

    Standard & Poor's Register of Corporations, Standard & Poor's Corp.

    American Business Directory (database), American Business Information

- For information on foreign-owned and international companies:

    International Directory of Corporate Affiliations, National Register Publishing Co.

    America's Corporate Families and International Affiliates, Dun & Bradstreet Information Services

    Directory of Foreign Manufacturers in the United States, Georgia State University Press

    Directory of Foreign Investment in the US, Gale Research Inc.

- For information on publicly-owned companies:

    Million Dollar Directory, Dun & Bradstreet Information Services

    Standard & Poor's Register of Corporations, Directors, and Executives, Standard & Poor's Corp.

Thomas Register of American Manufacturers, Thomas Publishing Co. (also available online at http://www.thomasregister.com/)

Ward's Business Directory of US Private and Public Companies, Gale Research Inc.

- For information on private companies:

    Directory of Leading Private Companies, National Register Publishing Co.

    Ward's Business Directory of US Private and Public Companies, Gale Research Inc.

- For information on fast-growing companies:

    International Business, "100 Fastest-Growing International Companies" (annual issue)

    Business Week, "100 Best Small Companies" (annual issue)

    Fortune, "100 Fastest-Growing Companies" (annual issue)

    Forbes, "200 Best Small Companies" (annual issue)

    Inc., "100 Fastest-Growing Public Companies" and "500 Most Rapidly Growing Private Companies" (annual issues)

- For specialized business directories (industrial, research & technology, advertising dollars, public relations information, etc.):

    Directories in Print, Gale Research Inc.

- For listings of small, local, or regional companies:

    State business, industrial, or manufacturing directories

    Chamber of Commerce directory

    Economic/Industrial Development Corporation directory

    Local and regional periodical and newspaper articles

    Personal contacts—business and community leaders

    Better Business Bureau

    Your local Yellow Pages

- For more detailed information on companies:

    Moody's Manuals, Moody's Investors Service, Inc.—brief history, business lines and products, properties, subsidiaries, financial statements, status of stocks and bonds

    Annual reports—financial data, current performance, future directions

    10K reports—business data, properties owned or leased, litigation pending, shareholder voting, management profiles, major stockholder profiles

    Business Periodicals Index, H.W. Wilson Co.—articles in business periodicals

    Predicasts F&S Index United States, Predicasts, Inc.—articles in trade journals, business newspapers, financial publications, and special reports

    Investment Service and Brokerage reports—financial and investment information

    Published histories

    Industry or association surveys

    Personal contacts

- For information on top executives:

  Standard & Poor's Register of Corporations, Directors, and Executives, Standard & Poor's Corp.

  Reference Book of Corporate Management, Dun & Bradstreet Information Services

  Who's Who in Finance and Industry, Marquis Who's Who Biennial

  Personal and professional contacts

- For industry information:

  Standard & Poor's Industry Surveys, Standards & Poor's Corp.

  U.S. Industrial Outlook, U.S. Department of Commerce

  Encyclopedia of Associations, Gale Research Inc.—for specific trade associations

  Professional association contacts

- For salary information:

  The American Almanac of Jobs and Salaries, Avon Books

  American Salaries and Wages Survey, Gale Research Inc.

  Occupational wage surveys, U.S. Bureau of Labor Statistics

  Trade journals and associations

  State employment offices

  Personal contacts

  JobSmart Salary Surveys—http://jobsmart.org/tools/salary/index.htm

  Relocation Salary Calculator—
  http://www.homefair.com/homefair/cmr/salcalc.html

- For geographic or relocation information:

  Places Rated Almanac, Prentice-Hall

  The Rating Guide to Life in America's Small Cities, Prometheus Books

  Chambers of Commerce

  Visitors' bureaus

  Local newspapers

  Realtors

  CityNet—http://www.city.net/

  CityLink—http://www.NeoSoft.com:80/citylink/

- For information on career fields or internships, or for general employment opportunity information:

  Occupational Outlook Handbook, U.S. Bureau of Labor Statistics

  The Encyclopedia of Career and Vocational Guidance, J.G. Ferguson Publishing Co.

  Internships, Peterson's Guides

  CPC Annual, College Placement Council

  Dun's Employment Opportunities Directory/The Career Guide, Dun & Bradstreet Information Services

  The National Job Bank, Bob Adams, Inc. (which also publishes numerous editions of regional Job Bank books for specific states or major metropolitan areas)

Peterson's Business and Management Jobs and *Peterson's Engineering, Science and Computer Jobs*, Peterson's Guides
Job Hunters Sourcebook, Gale Research Inc.
Personal contacts

- For executive recruiters:
  The Directory of Executive Recruiters, Kennedy Publications
  Personal contacts

- For current job postings:
  National Business Employment Weekly, Dow Jones & Co.
  National Ad Search, National Ad Search
  Trade journals
  Professional and trade associations
  College and university placement centers
  State employment services
  Newspapers and business periodicals
  Employer job hotlines
  Career Magazine—http://www.careermag.com/careermag/
  CareerMosaic—http://www.careermosaic.com
  E-Span—http://www.espan.com/
  The Monster Board–http://www.monster.com/
  Career Path—http://CareerPath.com

- Online and Internet resources not otherwise classified: (Note that this list is not comprehensive, but it will get you started on using the Internet to obtain information that will move your search along.)
  Yahoo—http://www.yahoo.com/   An indexed list of linked Internet sites. Type in a keyword for the information you are seeking, and Yahoo will search for sites that contain those words. You will then be able to go directly to the sites of interest to you.
  WebCrawler—http://webcrawler.com   A search engine for information on the World Wide Web only, but searchable by keywords.
  Tradewave.Galaxy—http://galaxy.tradewave.com   Searchable index to business and commercial Internet sites.
  Clearinghouse for Subject-Oriented Internet Resource Guides—http://www.clearinghouse.net   A comprehensive, searchable index to all kinds of Internet guides.
  Commercial Sites Index from Open Market—http://www.directory.net/   A searchable list of over 19,000 commercial organizations on the Internet.
  Hoover's On-Line—http://www.hoovers.com   A searchable database with company profiles plus links to other information resources related to the company.
  The Riley Guide—http://www.dbm.com/jobguide/   Overall, the best guide to the constantly changing career information sources on the Internet. Gives access information for want ads, resume databases, company information, and other items of interest to job seekers.

JobWeb—http://www/jobweb.org   A comprehensive career planning and employment information site.

RPI Career Resources—http://www.rpi.edu/dept/cdc/homepage.html A collection of links to U.S. and international resources.

General Note. Internet resources are changing and expanding at an extremely fast rate. Some of our recommendations may be obsolete or have different addresses by the time you read this. Utilize the major search engines supplied by your Internet service provider to find new and updated sources of information for your job search.

Practice Your Research Skills

Specific Organization Research

Your next step is to identify specific organizations that offer opportunities to do the kind of work that you want to do and to learn as much as you can about these organizations. Choose one organization to investigate and answer these questions.

Organization name: _____

Location: _____

What are the main products/services? _____

_____

How large is the organization? _____

Number of employees? _____ Profits in sales or number of people served? ___

_____

Publicly owned/privately owned/government? _____

For profit/nonprofit? _____

Financial data: _____

_____

What is the philosophy/culture/reputation? (e.g., Do they promote from within? Have high quality standards? Manage by teams?) _____

_____

_____

_____

What problems/challenges is the organization facing? _____

_____

_____

How has the organization responded to difficulties? _____

_____

_____

_____

(continued)

WORKSHEET 5.1

Continued.

Who are the top managers? _____

_____

How is the employee morale? _____

_____

Are the salaries competitive within the industry? _____

_____

What are some specific job titles of interest to you? _____

_____

_____

Who do I know who works for this organization? _____

_____

_____

Who do I know who might know someone who works for this organization?

_____

_____

_____

Field Research

One of the best ways to research your specific career field and jobs within it is to talk with people who actually work in the field or who interact with people who work in the field. Sometimes this is called "informational interviewing." You might think of it as "conversations with a purpose" or "field research." This type of research is especially helpful to someone who is new to full-time work, who is planning a career change of any magnitude, or for someone who is considering starting a business. You will be able to uncover potential resources, problems, and other information that you might not otherwise be able to find. To conduct field research, you will meet with someone who you think does the kind of work that you would like to do or someone who works in a closely related field. You are not looking for a job yet; you must be clear on this. Your purpose in talking with these people is to find out as much as you can about their work, in order for you to decide if you want to continue to pursue that field, to make some effective network contacts, and to get ideas about how to land a job in that field.

After you have conducted library research into your field of choice and have some basic information, you can begin to make a list of people to contact for your field research. You can find names through your own network of friends and colleagues, through business directories, or through association directories. Keep in mind that your best picture will emerge from talking with different people who know the field in a variety of ways. For example, if you are thinking of developing a training course to sell and deliver to businesses, you should talk to trainers, human resource professionals in the businesses that would be your target market, and account managers for training firms—the folks who sell training programs. From talking with these people, you will understand what kinds of programs businesses are seeking, the issues involved in selling training programs, and the issues involved in presenting programs to customers.

The thought of talking to strangers may be very scary for you. You may fear that they will resent the intrusion or that you will be refused or embarrassed. Usually, though, if you have done enough homework beforehand, so that you are knowledgeable about your topic, and if you hold to an agreed-upon amount of time for the interview, you will find that your request will be granted. In fact, your contact may be very flattered that you thought highly enough of her expertise to interview her.

You can practice this skill by trying out a nonthreatening interview with a friend. Try asking your friend about his favorite hobby or recreational activity. In ten minutes, ask enough questions to discover as much as you can about the activity. For example, ask how he got started, how often he does it, how he became interested, and with whom he does it. Write down everything you discover in the space on the following page.

Practice Interview:

_____

_____

_____

_____

_____

_____

_____

_____

_____

_____

_____

_____

_____

_____

_____

_____

_____

_____

_____

_____

_____

_____

_____

_____

_____

_____

_____

_____

Field Research Practice

Now that you've had some practice, prepare for a job-related field research interview in your field of interest. Gather your basic information and then develop a list of questions you feel will give you the kind of information you need to evaluate fully the particular job or career field. It is extremely important to think about this and plan your questions before you get in an interview! A prepared list will help you keep the interview moving, will show that you have already put some thought into your career planning, and will help keep you on track so you don't forget to ask crucial questions. The following is a suggested form to use to get you started on questions. Add questions that are important to you, and remove any questions that you don't feel are important.

1. How did you get started in this field?

   _____

   _____

   _____

2. What is your typical day/week like?

   _____

   _____

   _____

3. What kind of education or training does one need for this field?

   _____

   _____

   _____

4. What are your typical duties and responsibilities?

   _____

   _____

   _____

5. What are other jobs related to this field?

   _____

   _____

   _____

6. What kinds of employers offer these jobs?

   _____

   _____

   _____

(continued)

WORKSHEET 5.2

Continued.

7. What is an entry-level salary range in this area of the country?

_____

_____

_____

8. Are there opportunities to be self-employed in this field?

_____

_____

_____

9. What are some typical problems or difficulties that you encounter?

_____

_____

_____

10. Do you have any suggestions as to how I could move into this field based on my background?

_____

_____

_____

11. Is there anyone else that you would recommend that I talk with?

_____

_____

_____

Your additional questions:

_____

_____

_____

_____

_____

NETWORKING

BUILD A NETWORK, FIND A JOB

During your job search, almost everyone will come upon the advice to use "networking" to find a job. Research has shown that up to 80 percent of all jobs are found informally through networking versus formally through want ads, placement agencies, trade journals, personnel offices, or other formal mechanisms. The networking approach to job seeking involves talking with people such as friends, professional colleagues, and direct contacts. In the context of job searching, networking means a process of providing information about your job search goals and receiving advice, suggestions, and referrals that will help you reach your goals. You begin with people who already know you and then build a chain of contacts referred to you by your friends and colleagues.

The purpose of networking is to extend your eyes and ears to increase the number of job leads that you uncover. You tell your friends, acquaintances, and business associates exactly what kind of job you are seeking, and ask them for advice on how to uncover leads. Most importantly, you then ask for the names of people that they know who might be able to give you further advice. For networking to work properly, it is critical for you to be able to communicate your Ideal Position in a succinct manner.

Some job seekers think that they should network only with the hiring decision makers. This is not true. There are many people who do not have the power to hire, but have valuable information, advice, and referrals to share with you. For example, your next door neighbor, who is an administrative assistant for the sales and marketing department, does not have the authority to hire you in the accounting department. However, she probably does have valuable information to share with you about the organization, its culture, and who to talk to in the accounting department.

A network can grow quite quickly. For example, if you start with only five initial contacts who each give you advice and then three referrals, you now have 15 additional people in your network. If each of these contacts gives you three more names, you now have a *total* of 65 people who are aware of your job search and might be able to help you find a great job opening.

Whom should you contact? Begin with people you already know in a variety of ways, for example:

- Friends
- Neighbors
- Family and extended family members
- Business associates
- Salespeople
- Small business owners
- Religious leaders
- Professional advisors such as lawyers, CPAs
- Community leaders
- Professional association members
- College placement personnel and alumni
- Teachers
- Customers
- Competitors
- Everyone on your holiday greeting card list

Many job seekers are uncomfortable with the networking process of asking friends, professional colleagues, and strangers for help during their job search. You will find, though, that almost everyone you contact will be willing to give you information, advice, and referrals if approached with a few professional courtesies in mind:

- Have a clear objective of not only your job target or Ideal Position, but also the type of information, advice, or referral that you are seeking.
- When calling someone, be sure to ask if this is a convenient time to talk. If it is not convenient, then ask for a time to call again.
- Be sure to mention who referred you. Your mutual friend is the link between you and the referral that will "break the ice" and promote a willingness to help.
- Be sure *not* to ask directly for a job. This is not the purpose of networking. Explain that you are job hunting and would like advice on your search. For example, which companies are the best prospects for your particular job goal, who might be a good source of further information, and is there anything you should do to improve your search efforts?
- Prepare for your networking visit with as much care as you would a job interview. Dress appropriately, arrive on time, bring your resume, and be prepared to ask specific questions.
- Thank your network contact and ask if you may call again. You may want to write a brief thank-you note after you get off the phone or finish your meeting with the contact.

- Keep detailed records of your networking calls. Include dates and times of calls, phone numbers and addresses, and correct spellings of companies' and individuals' names. Take notes of the information gathered during a call or meeting.

- Stay in touch with your network contacts periodically. Diligent networkers can uncover many leads within a short time period that otherwise would never have surfaced.

- Once you find employment, write or call your network contacts to share the good news. Thank them again for their assistance during your search. Offer to assist them in the future in any way you can.

- Maintain your network after your search. During your job seeking, you tapped into your network and developed new contacts as well. Now that you are employed, spend some time and effort maintaining this valuable asset.

- Be available as a network contact to others. This is your opportunity to thank your contacts for their help.

Remember, networking during your job search can lead you to information, advice, and referrals that are invaluable to you. Again, there are many jobs that are never advertised because they are filled through personal referrals. Try putting the power of networking to work for you.

Let's imagine how a networking call might sound:

"John, my name is Sue Storch. I am a friend of Mary Jones, who knows you from the Personnel Association."

"Oh yes. Mary and I worked on a committee together last year. She has such a high level of positive energy!"

"You're right about that. Talking to Mary always makes me feel optimistic. John, the reason I am calling is to see if you might be able to help me with my job search."

"Gee, Sue. Our company just let a number of people go. I'm afraid I can't help you."

"Oh, I didn't mean that you would know of a job. What I'm looking for is advice, and the names of people I should be talking with."

"Oh, okay. Tell me about your background."

"I've been personnel administrator in a small sales office for the last four years. I do the payroll, administer benefits, develop policies, and handle all the employee relations functions. My office is being moved out of state, and I don't want to relocate, so I'm looking for new opportunities. Do you have any suggestions about what I should do?"

"Well, it sounds to me like you could be an HR generalist in a larger firm, or look for a similar position to what you have now. Do you want to stay in a sales office?"

"Not necessarily. In fact, I think I'd like to get into a larger organization where I'd have some new challenges."

"Are you a member of the Personnel Association?"

"Yes, but I haven't been very active."

"I suggest you attend the next meeting. I plan to go, and I could introduce you to a number of people there who are HR generalists and who could give you more information. You know, they also have a 'Job Hotline' that's updated every week. It usually includes generalist jobs. You might also volunteer for the upcoming Job Summit. I know they need a lot of help with that, and you'll meet a lot of people from all over the area."

"John, those are excellent ideas. I will be at the next meeting; in fact, I plan to attend with Mary. In the meantime, can you think of anyone else I should talk with who might be able to help me?"

"Let me give you the phone number of Jeff Stone. He's a trainer who gets into a lot of different companies with his program, and he might know of some companies that are hiring."

"John, thanks again. You've been extremely helpful. I'll contact Jeff and I'll let you know what he tells me. I will see you at the next meeting, then."

Sue got lots of good advice and a referral once she reassured John that she didn't expect him to find a job for her within his company. She'll have an opportunity to meet him face to face at the meeting, and that will firm up their relationship. Sue will be able to contact John again for further advice and referrals.

Does networking work? Yes, it definitely is a job search strategy that you will want to use. The reason that it works is that you are being referred by someone who knows you and your capabilities. You are also tapping into others' contacts and ideas. Eventually, you will begin to talk to people who know of specific job opportunities that will be right for you.

How do you get started? First, make a list of networking contacts. Next, determine what you want to say. Next, begin making your calls. And, be sure to keep detailed records.

My Network List

Make a list of people you want to contact regarding your job search. At this time, list everyone you can think of without evaluating the quality of the contact. You never know who may know someone or know someone who knows someone. The elderly neighbor next door may have a son who is the president of a company for which you would love to work.

EXAMPLE

NAME	CONNECTION
Jane Smith	ASTD President
Mary Jones	HR Association member
Bob Gold	Neighbor; works at Smith Shipping Company

Networking Contact Sheet

Name _____

Title _____

Company _____

Address _____

Phone number _____ E-mail _____

Relationship _____

Describe contact (call, meeting, referral) _____

_____

_____

_____

_____

Results or action taken based on contact _____

_____

_____

_____

_____

Network Script

Use the form below to lay out information that you want to be sure to share with your contact. It is not necessary to memorize your script but instead use it as a guideline. You want to listen carefully to your contact's information and respond appropriately.

Introduction:

Hello, _____ , my name is _____

I was referred to you by _____

Explanation:

I was talking to _____ about my job search, and he/she suggested that you might be able to give me some information or suggestions that would be helpful to me. Let me assure you that I don't expect you to find a job for me; I'm hoping that you will be able to give me the names of employers, associations, or individuals I can talk with that might help me find some good leads.

My Ideal Position would be to find a job doing _____

_____

This is what I have done so far _____

_____

_____

I would like to know more about _____

_____

Do you have any suggestions for me, or names of other people to talk with who might be

able to help me? _____

Close:

Thank you so much for taking time to help me. I will definitely contact these people and organizations. Is it okay if I contact you in the future to update you on my progress or to ask further questions?

TELEPHONE PROSPECTING

Telephone prospecting is a critical job search strategy. Mastering this technique will open the door to many opportunities that you would not necessarily encounter in other ways. Simply stated, it consists of four main steps:

- identifying employers of interest to you
- identifying the decision maker or hiring authority at each organization
- developing a telephone prospecting script
- calling the appropriate individual to set up an appointment

The purpose of telephone prospecting is to schedule an appointment with the person in charge of the department or area in which you want to work. In job seeking, nothing happens until you have an opportunity to meet with the person who has the power to hire. Often openings are created for those who impress the hiring authority, even when specific openings did not exist before the interview. The telephone is an efficient and effective means of scheduling appointments that are critical to your job search.

Studies have shown that more people find employment through people they know and by directly contacting employers than by any other means. Many companies announce available positions internally to encourage in-house promotion, avoid advertising costs, and to permit a more thorough evaluation of candidates. As a result, there are many jobs that are available within an organization that never reach a newspaper want ad.

Benefits of Telephone Prospecting

Using the telephone is a convenient, effective means of uncovering opportunities and setting up meetings with the people who have information and authority regarding hiring decisions. We have worked with hundreds of job hunters throughout the country who have affirmed that telephone prospecting was an invaluable technique in their job search. The most difficult part of this technique to many individuals is overcoming the fear of picking up the phone and making calls. Effective preparation, confidence in your abilities and what you have to offer, and a positive attitude are necessary for successful job prospecting.

Telephone Prospecting Steps

First, let's look at the telephone prospecting steps leading to the identification of the person to whom you wish to speak and the development of an individually tailored script.

1. *Identify prospective employers.* From your job search research, develop a list of employers you want to contact. Keep your list manageable by starting with 15 to 20 employers, working through the list, and if necessary, adding more companies to your list.

2. *Target your call.* Unless you already have the name of a specific person to speak to, you should first obtain the name of the decision maker or hiring authority for your area of expertise. Usually this information can be

obtained through an initial phone call to the receptionist at the company's main number. You might say:

> *"Hello, could you tell me the name of the person in charge of (position you are seeking)? How is that spelled? What is her/his title? Does she/he have a direct dial number? Thank you."*

or

> *"I would like to send some information to the person in charge of (functional area). Could you please tell me who that is?"*

Be sure to check title, spelling, and ask for the extension or direct line number and e-mail address.

It is important to note here that you are not asking for information on the personnel or human resources manager, but instead the person in charge of the department or area in which you would work. The human resources department is usually focused on current openings and may not even be aware of jobs that may be developing. It is very common for this department to respond by requesting that you send a resume for their file or by telling you there are no immediate openings. This is the response that you are attempting to avoid. You are interested in talking to the person who could make an immediate hiring decision about jobs that are developing or about possible personnel changes *before this information ever reaches the personnel department.*

3. *Develop your script.* As much as possible, individualize your script for the particular organization or company that you are contacting.

Identify yourself:

> *"Hello, Ms. Jones, my name is _____.*
> *I'm with Waterloo Products."*

or

> *"Hello, my name is _____. Lindsay Selkirk*
> *suggested I call you."*

Reason for calling:

> *"I am a mechanical engineer with a background in total quality management. I am familiar with your company's reputation for quality, and I am interested in exploring opportunities to become involved with your TQM program."*

or

> *"I am a recent graduate in Business Administration, and I am exploring career opportunities in the accounting field."*

Overview of qualifications:

> *"My background includes ten years in the area of manufacturing with experience in all aspects of quality control."*

Ask for an appointment:

"I would like to make an appointment to meet with you briefly to introduce myself personally and discuss opportunities. Would tomorrow afternoon or next Thursday work for you?"

4. *Make your calls.* Set goals and dedicate time to make calls each day.

Telephone Prospecting Tips

- Develop an individually tailored script. Using the Telephone Prospecting Script forms on the following pages, develop your script based on your background and accomplishments.
- Practice your script. Read your script aloud to determine how it sounds. Refine it if necessary. Call a friend and ask him or her to listen to your script and give you feedback.
- Refine your script. After practicing your script and soliciting feedback from others, revise your script, making any necessary changes or improvements.
- Stop now and complete the telephone prospecting sheet on the next page. There are extra sheets for you to use with different employers or different situations.

Telephone Prospecting Script

Identify Yourself

"Hello, _____ , my name is _____ .

I'm with _____ ."

or

"I have been referred by _____ ."

Reason for Calling

_____

_____

_____

_____

_____

Overview of Qualifications

(You may want to use your career summary here or talk about one or two specific accomplishments.)

_____

_____

_____

_____

_____

Ask for the Appointment

_____

_____

_____

_____

_____

Telephone Prospecting Script

Identify Yourself

"Hello, ———————————— , my name is ———————————— .

I'm with ————————————————————————."

or

"I have been referred by ————————————————————."

Reason for Calling

————————————————————————————————

————————————————————————————————

————————————————————————————————

————————————————————————————————

————————————————————————————————

Overview of Qualifications

(You may want to use your career summary here or talk about one or two specific accomplishments.)

————————————————————————————————

————————————————————————————————

————————————————————————————————

————————————————————————————————

Ask for the Appointment

————————————————————————————————

————————————————————————————————

————————————————————————————————

————————————————————————————————

Tips for Successful Prospecting

- Plan your work and work your plan. Develop a list of the calls that you want to make, start calling, and don't stop until you have worked through the entire list.
- Call early in the morning and late in the afternoon. These are excellent times to reach people in their offices.
- Practice your script. Make it conversational. Revise it as necessary for each organization or prospect.
- Smile. Relax. Remember, you have something to offer the employer. Be confident.
- Follow up with your promises; for example, send your resume or call again next Friday.
- Recognize your apprehensions. Don't wait until you are comfortable to make calls. The more calls you make, the easier it becomes.
- As the Nike commercial advocates, "Just do it." Don't delay, procrastinate, or think you have a better way. Calling is the most effective strategy for reaching potential employers.
- Beware of "rocky shoals;" learn to overcome objections.

Regardless of how skilled you are on the telephone, there are times when you *will* run into a rocky shoal. Here are some responses that will help you through some possible difficulties.

What to do if the person you want to meet with says:

"Send me your resume."

> *"I would be delighted to send you my resume, but I would like to introduce myself personally to you. Would it be possible to meet with you for just 15 or 20 minutes? I promise not to take much of your time."*

or

> *"I will be in your area next week. Could I drop off my resume at that time?"*

"We have no openings."

> *"I understand that you may not have any openings at this time, but you never know when something will open up. I would like to meet with you and learn more about your organization."*

"The position has been filled."

> *"I am sorry to hear that, as I was looking forward to the possibility of working for your company. I am still interested in meeting with you and discussing any future openings."*

or

> *"I am still interested in meeting with you to get your ideas and suggestions to help me with my job search."*

Working with Administrative Staff

You'll soon find that sometimes your call will be routed to an administrative assistant. You need a strategy to work effectively with this individual.

Keep in mind that part of an administrative assistant's job may be to screen distracting calls. You still want your call to get through, but you must respect this person's function.

As with any contact you make, be polite and courteous, and create a positive impression of yourself. Several possible scenarios might occur:

- You are asked for your name and organization. Respond with your name, and, if possible, immediately mention that you were referred to your contact. That alone may smooth the way for you if the administrator knows your referring party.

- You are asked the reason that you are calling. Be brief, and indicate that you are calling for advice and counsel on a matter related to your field of work.

- You are told that your contact is not in. Rather than leave a message, ask when you might be able to call back and reach your contact. This allows you to maintain control over the call. If you leave a message, your contact may call back when you are not available or at an inconvenient time.

- You have tried repeatedly to call your contact and never got through. Try calling an hour before or after regular office hours. That way, you may avoid the staff and get right to your contact.

What to Do with Voice Mail

When confronted by voice mail, listen carefully to the message. You might be told exactly the best time to call. If not, leave a message with your referring party's name and indicate you'll call back. After trying two or three times to get through, try a new approach. Leave a message with your number and a suggested time to reach you. Briefly explain that you are seeking advice and information only. After two days, if you have not received a call back, try calling the main number of the organization, follow directions to speak to an operator, and say:

> *"I'm so glad to speak to a live person. I'm afraid I may not be using the phone system properly. I have been trying to contact .... for a few days, and I keep getting lost in the system. Could you please connect me directly?"*

If that doesn't work, go back to your referral and ask for assistance in making the contact. If you do not have a referral, try to give the person a reason to talk with you. For example, mention a newspaper article about the company, or mention their reputation in the area as the reason you are calling. Try sending a letter first, then following with a call. Unfortunately, you may run into someone who uses voice mail as a moat across which no strangers may pass. If that's the case, move on.

Mastering the telephone will greatly increase the number of contacts you are able to make and the efficiency of your job search. You will find that the phone can be one of your best navigational aids during your job search journey.

7

YOUR CORRESPONDENCE

A SIMPLE APPROACH TO WRITING EFFECTIVE COVER LETTERS

One of the frequently dreaded tasks in job hunting is writing cover letters. Whether it is composing a cover letter written in response to a want ad or a prospecting letter written directly to an employer of interest, letter-writing often produces anxiety. It isn't surprising that it does. Most people rarely write social letters any more since the telephone makes instant communication easy. And even though many people write memos and letters regularly in their work, somehow a letter about one's self is much harder to compose than a letter about a business matter.

In fact, a letter written during your job search is very important, no matter what stage of the job search process you are in. If written in response to an ad, your letter may have to compete with several hundred others to catch the eye of the reader, who will probably go on to review your resume only if your cover letter is interesting. Even a letter written directly to a specific person may be competing with hundreds of other prospecting letters arriving each day to that company.

It's not surprising that the second largest collection of books in the career section of the library is on how to write cover letters. Many job hunters thumb through these guides looking for an example of a letter which most closely resembles their situation and then copy it word for word. Unfortunately, the letter usually reads like it was copied out of a book. Use guides to get ideas about format, organization, and different approaches, but then try writing your own letter using a three-paragraph format which answers three basic questions.

First Paragraph
Why am I writing?

If you are writing in response to an ad, mention the heading or title, the newspaper or journal in which it was published, and the date it ran. Then briefly describe what caught your eye in the ad that made you decide to respond.

If you are prospecting, mention why you have chosen to contact that particular organization or person. You may know something about the organization from networking or from an article in a newspaper or journal. Mention the source of your interest. It doesn't hurt to use some flattery here, if you are sincere.

Second Paragraph
What do I have that you need?

If the ad includes a list of requirements that a candidate must have, respond with your own list of how you meet those requirements. It is a good idea to list them in the same order as they appear in the ad. If you meet the requirements exactly, it is especially effective to make a two-column section, with their requirements in the left column, matched by your qualities in the right column directly opposite. This is called a "balance sheet" approach.

EXAMPLE

JOB REQUIREMENTS	MY QUALIFICATIONS
■ College degree	■ BS in business
■ 5 years' experience in accounting	■ 6 years as staff accountant
■ Knowledge of accounting software	■ Proficient in Quickbooks and Peachtree Accounting

In the prospecting letter, this second paragraph is your chance to present information you have learned about the organization that leads you to think that it could use someone with your talents. You may have gathered this information through research, informational interviewing, or through articles in the area press. You might use a referral's name here.

In either situation, don't simply repeat what is in your resume. Tailor your information for this specific opportunity instead. Your task is to interest the reader in looking closely at your resume. You have something important to offer: your unique set of talents and skills. Be proud of yourself, and let it show in your letter.

Third Paragraph
Where do we go from here?

Close the letter with a positive, assertive statement. "I look forward to speaking with you about this opportunity" is much stronger than "I hope to hear from you soon." Make it clear that you expect to advance past the initial screening process.

In a prospecting situation, you may want to indicate a time when you will call to discuss your ideas and their opportunities. In fact, any time you have the contact information, take control of the follow-up process and indicate that you will call to discuss the next step. Then be sure to do it!

Above all, keep your letters simple and straightforward. Don't try to sound sophisticated by including words that you do not normally use. You may use them incorrectly. Do not sprinkle in words like "herewith" and "theretofore" for effect. Write a bit more formally than you would speak, and you'll sound natural and sincere. Check the spelling and grammar in your letter and ask someone else to review it. Your first letter will be the hardest, but you can then use it as a basic guide for other letters of the same type.

A Simple Approach to Writing Effective Thank-You Letters

Sending a thank-you note following an interview or meeting helps you to be remembered and appreciated. If someone has assisted you, send a thank-you note. Many job seekers forget this business nicety, which can make you stand out from the crowd. Follow these general tips and remember to keep your thank-you note simple and brief.

- It is perfectly acceptable to handwrite your thank-you note. In fact, it may make it seem more personal.
- Send a thank-you note immediately after each job interview or networking or prospecting appointment. You may want to send one even after a valuable telephone conversation you have with someone.
- Address it specifically and correctly to the person you want to thank. You can write "Confidential" on the lower left corner of the envelope.
- Open your note by thanking the person for the meeting, appointment, or interview and his or her time, advice, and/or assistance.
- Emphasize a highlight or two from your meeting.
- If you think there is something that you wish you had discussed during the interview or meeting but forgot, mention it now. For example, *"I neglected to mention that I am proficient with a number of computer software packages."*
- Close the note with a reminder of your plan for your next contact. For example, *"As agreed, I will be calling you again in early December."*

In the next section, there are a series of cover letter examples for different job search situations, an example of a networking letter, and an example of a thank-you letter sent after a job interview.

PAULA BROWN

919 North Street   **Newton, MA 02386**   **(508) 555-3456**

April 15, 2000

Rockland Trust Company
Human Resources Department
288 Union Street
Rockland, MA 02370
Attention: Raymond Fuerschbach

Dear Mr. Fuerschbach:

I am writing in response to your advertisement for a Budget Analyst in the *Boston Globe* on Sunday, April 10. I am familiar with Rockland Trust; in fact, my good friend Joe Forgione is a vice president in the Commercial Banking Division. After reading the requirements for the position, I felt that my background and experience were a good match for your needs. I have summarized your requirements and my experience below.

> YOU REQUIRE: 5–10 years' experience; BS/MBA
> Proven budgeting experience
> Strong time management skills
> Strong communication skills
> Strong PC skills
> Report writing experience

> I HAVE: 10+ years' experience; MBA—Pepperdine U.
> Budgeting experience in several industries
> Proven ability to manage complex projects and meet deadlines
> Proven ability to consult with people in a variety of departments/levels
> Hands-on experience with PC and mainframe analysis computing
> Experience writing a wide variety of management reports

In addition, I have been involved in budget preparation and budget management in both banking and telecommunications. Much of my time has been spent working closely with a wide range of departments within my organizations to develop variance reporting procedures to improve the accuracy of forecasting.

I am very interested in discussing this position with you. I look forward to talking with you soon.

Sincerely yours,

Paula Brown
Enclosure

WANT-AD RESPONSE

LOIS LANE
69 Rolling Plains
Wilshire, NY 12837
(518) 585-4463
loislane@evergreen.net

November 21, 1999

Grain's Lansing Business
592 E. Broadway
Lansing, MI 48732
Attention: Barry White, Publisher

Dear Mr. White:

An important business publication such as *Grain's Lansing Business* requires advertising account managers with a track record of success. I am an experienced sales professional with a strong record of success. I am currently seeking a new opportunity and am interested in speaking with you about your publication's needs.

In my current position, I make both appointments and cold calls to prospective customers. My conversion rate is 75% on my cold calls. I develop and make formal sales presentations to my prospects and work closely with them to determine their specific needs. I formulate specific campaigns and strategies based on their marketing needs and budget. Further, I maintain and service all of my accounts, including resolving credit problems. I have an outstanding record of performance in meeting quotas, developing new accounts, and increasing sales revenues.

I would like to meet with you to discuss any sales opportunities that you have in your organization where my experience and skills can help you meet your sales goals. I will contact you soon to set up an appointment. I appreciate your consideration in reviewing my qualifications and I look forward to meeting with you soon.

Best regards,

Lois Lane

Enclosure

PROSPECTING LETTER

DUKE HAZZARD

5 Boss Road
Kingstown, NY 12844

(518) 766-0444 (Home)
(518) 744-5805 (Work)

November 5, 1999

Semper Claims Group
PO Box 12345
Albany, NY 12212-2345
Attention: Kermit Leach, Claims Manager

Dear Mr. Leach:

Your advertisement for **Insurance Claim Supervisor** in the Sunday, October 22 *Times Union* caught my eye. As an experienced supervisor and adjuster for a major insurance company, I am confident that I have the skills and experience that you are seeking.

Your ad indicated the need for an applicant experienced in both maintenance claims and supervision. You also indicated the desire for someone with a bachelor's degree who is PC literate. I have over ten years' experience in the insurance industry. For the past year, I have been a litigation adjuster, investigating, monitoring, and settling claims that have gone into litigation or are likely to. I have worked closely with defense counsel, outside adjusters, and claimants and have a strong record of successful resolution of claims. Prior to this position, I supervised five inside and outside liability adjusters. In this role, I controlled case assignments and reserves and approved settlements. I also served my entire branch in several coordinator roles requiring close communications with other supervisors and special risk clients.

I completed a four-year degree in Criminal Justice at the University of Illinois at Chicago. I am PC literate and I have excellent writing skills.

I look forward to speaking with you about the positions that are open. Thank you for your consideration in reviewing my application.

Sincerely yours,

Duke Hazzard

Enclosure

WANT-AD RESPONSE

JOLENE CZERNY
1 King of Prussia Court
Sarasota Springs, FL 33869
(813) 481-5192

April 12, 2000

Microcomputers Worldwide
59325 E. Lake Washington Road
Seattle, WA 98135
Attention: Mr. William Gates, Logistics Director

Dear Mr. Gates:

I am interested in exploring any opportunities your organization might have in distribution services, warehouse operations, or logistics. As a logistics supervisor with over five years' combined experience in these areas, the last two in a supervisory role, I have repeatedly demonstrated my ability to operate an efficient and innovative department and have been responsible for significant cost savings.

One of the primary areas of cost savings in a high-volume sales organization such as Microcomputers Worldwide is constant attention to small details in logistics. As you can see in the enclosed resume, I have been able to visualize areas of opportunity and implement new programs and services to improve operations and realize savings. Because of my drive to constantly improve myself and my operation, I have had outstanding performance reviews in all of my positions. I enjoy working as part of a team, setting mutually beneficial goals, and I am also able to work effectively as a leader or supervisor.

I am currently interested in relocating to the Seattle area and have contacted you because of the fine reputation of your organization. I believe that I can make significant contributions to your department and your firm. I will contact you soon to discuss your current needs and opportunities.

Sincerely yours,

Jolene Czerny

Enclosure

PROSPECTING LETTER

PATRICIA DIMWORTH
4 Heath Lane
Memphis, TN 37866
(615) 538-1634
pdimworth@netgate.net

August 20, 2000

Tarkington Floor Products
1293 W. Main
Memphis, TN 37851
(615) 532-7893
Attention: Mary Armstrong, Director of Sales & Marketing

Dear Ms. Armstrong:

I am seeking a position in **sales** or **sales management** with your organization. I have a consistent record of success in sales and management within a variety of industries. I am looking for an opportunity to join a progressive employer where I can continue to develop and learn and provide high sales returns.

In my most recent position, I have been able to increase sales in my territories every year, in spite of economic slowdowns and difficult markets. I have built a high level of trust and loyalty with my customers, even as my territory size and complexity has increased. Unlike many manufacturing sales positions, I deal closely with both distributors and retailers, and am able to work effectively at all levels with people from different backgrounds. I have always been able to develop a thorough understanding of my products from manufacturing to distribution and sales and am able to convey that information effectively to my clients through training and product demonstrations.

I appreciate your consideration. I will contact you next week to discuss opportunities within your organization.

Sincerely,

Patricia Dimworth

Enclosure

PROSPECTING LETTER

STEVEN SPIELMAN
467 Woodchuck Hollow
Saranac Lake, NY 12567
(518) 498-2846 • Fax (518) 498-2847

May 25, 2000

Bethany Hospital
17 Woodridge Road
Woodridge, NJ 02731
Attention: Joan Fontana, Director of Nursing

Dear Ms. Fontana:

I am returning to New Jersey soon, after spending several years in upstate New York caring for my grandmother who has Alzheimer's disease. She is now entering a nursing facility, so I plan to look for permanent work. I am writing to explore opportunities as a mental health therapy aide or nurse's aide in your organization. I believe that my background and experience will interest you.

My most recent experience has been in mental healthcare. I have been the primary caregiver for my grandmother for the last two years. In this role, I have interviewed and hired respite workers, planned and prepared meals, supervised and accompanied her on outings, and provided physical care and therapy. Prior to assuming this responsibility, I worked in the mental health unit of the local hospital, evaluating patients, conducting group sessions, assisting in developing patient treatment plans, and providing daily care and therapy. I found that I enjoyed working with this type of patient.

I have the ability to give emotional support to my patients while still expecting them to participate in their treatment. I plan to return to school to obtain an associate's degree in Human Services and to become a Certified Alcohol and Substance Abuse Counselor. I have also worked as a nurse's aide in a variety of hospital departments as well as in private care. I am highly skilled, and I take pride in my work. I love to learn new things and continue to upgrade my skills and abilities.

I hope we can get together to discuss any opportunities you might have. I will contact you within two weeks to set up an appointment.

Sincerely yours,

Steven Spielman, CNA

Enclosure

PROSPECTING LETTER

DAMEON CELESTINE
264 Crescent Street
New Orleans, LA 70166
(504) 284-0437

March 12, 1999

R & L Beverages
PO Box 397
New Orleans, LA 70162
Attention: Roxanne Pepper, General Manager

Dear Ms. Pepper:

I recently completed a Bachelor's Degree in Business as a returning adult student. I concentrated on marketing and finance in my studies because I found through my prior small business and property owner experience that my interests and skills lay in those areas. I am now seeking a position in sales or management with an employer who can benefit by my willingness to work hard and contribute to growth.

I believe that I can bring a unique combination of skills to your organization. Not only do I have a proven track record of success in business, but I have also maintained a high grade average in my college studies while continuing to manage and renovate my rental properties and work part-time to support myself. I can bring to your organization not only enthusiasm and an ability to learn, but also a strong desire to succeed and an excellent understanding of the problems and opportunities facing a business.

Can we get together to discuss opportunities within your organization? I will contact you in about a week to set up an appointment. Thank you for your consideration.

Sincerely yours,

Dameon Celestine

Enclosure

PROSPECTING LETTER

LAUREN HUTTON
12 Sioux Trail
Fargo, ND 57908
(606) 327-9351

September 12, 1999

MegaWest Bank
2 Main Street
Fargo, ND 57912
Attention: James Bond, Executive Vice President

Dear Mr. Bond:

After many years of working closely with business and community leaders for the benefit of civic and charitable organizations, I am now seeking to use my experience and skills in a business setting. I am particularly interested in working in **fundraising, marketing,** and/or **public relations** in private banking or for a not-for-profit institution. The volunteer activities I have led have put me in close contact with powerful and influential people throughout the country. I know these individuals are critically important for the success of these businesses and I have demonstrated my ability to work for and with them.

I have developed excellent management skills through both work and volunteer experiences. I am particularly skilled at managing complex projects, working effectively with directors, staff, and contractors, and following projects through to successful completion. I have an extremely high energy level, and a desire to succeed, and I feel confident that I can learn new skills quickly and completely.

I am looking forward to a chance to meet with you personally to discuss opportunities at your organization. I will contact you soon to set up an appointment. Thank you for your consideration.

Sincerely yours,

Lauren Hutton

Enclosure

PROSPECTING LETTER

June 10, 1999

Merrill Dean Barney
12 Broadway
Denver, CO 80971
Attention: Louis Rook, Managing Director

Dear Mr. Rook:

Because you are a key member of one of the more prominent and respected brokerage firms in the greater Denver area, I am contacting you in the hope that you may be able to render some valuable suggestions and advice to help me make a successful career change into the investment brokerage field. Unlike most new graduates with degree in hand and no particular direction in mind, I know that this is the field that I want to enter. I have been building my knowledge base for the last few years as I completed my bachelor's degree, and I am now looking for an opportunity to join a well-respected firm that will open its doors to a determined, goal-oriented, mature newcomer.

Through launching a successful business beginning with extremely limited capital, I learned to take a long-range view of business and investments. As I built a strong customer base through reputation and referrals, I discovered the necessity of building trust and loyalty in my customers. Since completing my degree as a returning adult student, I understand the importance of setting and reaching goals. I believe that these qualities are necessary to be an investment broker who seeks to build a recurrent client base. I started an investment club while a student, for myself and other interested students, in order to learn more about financial investments and necessary strategies to foster a successful turnout. I have begun studying for the Series 7 licensing exam. The more I learn about this exciting field, the more I am convinced that this is exactly what I want to do.

I appreciate your consideration in reviewing my letter and resume. I would like a chance to meet with you to discuss your ideas and suggestions about entering this field. I will contact you by phone in about a week to schedule an appointment.

Sincerely yours,

Phillip R. Driver

Enclosure

PROSPECTING LETTER

CAROL O'FLAHERTY
395 Morgan Circle
Walnut Creek, CA 97023
(730) 597-2047
co'flaherty@aol.com

November 16, 1999

El Curtola Foods
937 Pleasanton Avenue
Contra Costa, CA 97154
Attention: Wayne Wong, Director of Quality Assurance

Dear Mr. Wong:

Thank you for giving me an opportunity to meet with you yesterday to discuss the position of Quality Assurance Supervisor in the Food Safety Laboratory. After talking with you, I have a much better understanding of the difficulties you are facing in gaining ISO 9000 certification.

As we discussed, I coordinated the ISO certification for the Del Rio Foods salami manufacturing plant over the past year and a half. The process was complicated and sometimes frustrating, but I found that I had a talent for bringing all the pieces of the puzzle together. In fact, I enjoyed the experience so much and learned so much from it that I am anxious to build on my skills in a larger food manufacturing setting like yours. Having so recently successfully managed the ISO process while supervising the QA lab at Del Rio, I am confident that I can do the same for you.

I understand that you will be making a final decision in two weeks. I want to emphasize to you that I am very interested in the position, and am excited about having a chance to help El Curtola Foods move forward with ISO certification. I look forward to hearing from you.

Sincerely yours,

Carol O'Flaherty

THANK YOU LETTER

JANICE JAMES
470 Holiday Lake Road
Louisville, KY 40284
(502) 897-4729

December 12, 2000

Mr. Chuck Jones
Track Superintendent
Churchill Downs
PO Box 495
Louisville, KY 40278

Dear Mr. Jones:

My friend, jockey Julie Mars, suggested that I write to you concerning my attempts to obtain a position as a trainer. I have recently moved to the Louisville area from upstate New York, where I have lived and worked for the last five years. I met Julie at the Saratoga Springs racetrack in 1991, and we have had a close friendship ever since.

In Saratoga, I served as apprentice trainer to Bill Johnson, head trainer for the Whitney Stables. I progressed to journeyman, then assistant trainer over the next three years. In 1997, I was given full responsibility for three of the Whitney thoroughbreds, all 2-year-old fillies. I was able to amass a winning season with all three. Because the owners of the stable decided to sell most of their stock, I decided to move down to Kentucky to take advantage of the milder climate and longer season. I am now trying to find a good opportunity as a trainer for a medium to large stable.

Julie felt that you would be able to give me some good advice on which stables to contact and, possibly, specific head trainers to meet. I would like to set up an appointment for a brief talk with you at your convenience to discuss the training opportunities in this region. I will contact you within a week to set up a time to meet. I appreciate any assistance or ideas you can give me.

Sincerely yours,

Janice James

SECTION THREE

SAILING AWAY

JOB SEARCH MANAGEMENT

You will progress more efficiently in your job search journey if you plan your daily and weekly activities, set goals, keep track of all of your contacts and appointments, and review your progress periodically.

Your primary tool for managing this journey is a personal calendar that will allow you to record appointments, follow-up calls, mileage records, and other information important to your search. Your next tool should be a filing system to organize your prospecting and networking contacts. This can be an index card file, a ring binder, a computer database management program, or some other system. These systems allow you one document per name, which can be sorted alphabetically for easy retrieval. You may also want to use a spreadsheet or contact tracker to record important events that occur with each contact, such as resumes sent, thank-you notes sent, and follow-up calls to make. We have included forms and schedules for you to use or adapt for use in the following pages. You may make as many copies of each as you require.

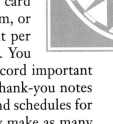

DEFINE YOUR GOALS

The majority of jobs are filled through networking or direct prospecting with employers. Some are filled by answering published ads, and the rest are filled through other sources. You should schedule your campaign to use the methods with the greatest payoff and to make the most efficient use of your time.

This means developing and following a structured, organized search every day. Develop a plan of action based on the most productive means of finding job leads. Research from various sources repeatedly shows that, on average, 90 percent of available jobs are filled through three sources:

Networking and prospecting—70 percent

Search firms or employment agencies—10 percent

Want ads—10 percent

Thus, job seekers should concentrate 70 percent of their time on networking and prospecting, 10 percent of their time contacting employment agencies or recruiters, and 10 percent of their time reading and answering want ads. The remaining 10 percent of time can be spent using other methods of uncovering leads.

If you are not currently working, your plan can be structured like this. Looking at a typical week, Sunday should be your primary day to review newspaper want ads and write response letters. You may wish to delay mailing your letters until Tuesday or later, however, since the bulk of the responses will be mailed on Monday. Your letter, mailed a day or two later, may get more notice since it will arrive in a smaller group of responses, and will be read after the others have been reviewed. Sunday evening, plan your calls to be made on Monday.

In general, on Monday through Friday, you should concentrate on making phone calls or going to interviews during business hours. Set a goal for yourself of a certain number of calls or interviews to make each day. Be realistic—you should be able to make between ten and twenty calls per day, but you probably won't be able to go to more than two or three interviews per day, considering travel time and other issues. If you have downtime while waiting for calls to be returned, you can review trade journals or other business publications for want ads and business news. On a normal weekday, you can begin phoning by 7:30 A.M. and continue until 5:30 P.M. with a break for lunch. You will be calling network contacts and employer prospects to arrange interviews, to arrange to send your resume, or to get ideas and referrals to other contacts. You can also use downtime between calls or while waiting for callbacks to write letters and plan for the next day.

Each week, you should schedule time to conduct research on prospective employers or to prepare for interviews. You may be able to do some of this at home via your computer or you may need to go to a library. The amount of time you spend will be determined by how much and what kind of information you are seeking.

You should also plan time each week to review your progress, organize your records, and plan for the next week. This can be done during downtime or on a weekday or Sunday evening.

DEVELOP YOUR PLAN

Take out your calendar and begin to plan your job search. Each week you should allot time for research, telephone calls, meetings, letter writing, and review of your progress and planning. Decide on a realistic amount of time to be given to each activity. Reserve most of the hours between 7:30 A.M. and 5:30 P.M. for telephone calls and meetings when people are usually in their offices. Fit your other activities into off hours, or when waiting for calls to be returned. You should plan on working 30 to 40 hours per week on your job search. Do not let other activities begin to encroach on this time. Set goals for yourself. For example:

Number of calls dialed per day

Number of calls completed per day

Number of meetings (field research, networking, job interviews) per week

Number of letters written (want ad response, direct contact) per week

Record your goals in a plan that you formulate at the beginning of each week. Remember that 70 percent of your time should be devoted to networking and prospecting efforts. If you plan to work for six hours every day, 4.2 hours should be concentrated on telephone calls, networking meetings, and networking letters, with the majority of your time spent directly talking with others.

Schedule a time at the end of the week to review your progress and make changes to your plan. Increase or reduce the target numbers as necessary, but always keep in mind that your best results will come from making those personal contacts.

Finally, you need to make sure that you schedule time for yourself, your family and friends, and for recreational activities. A job search is best accomplished by treating it as a full-time job, but it shouldn't consume your life. Try to keep a balance in your life. You need to keep a perspective about your search in terms of your life management goals and needs.

If you are already employed, your job search will have to fit into available hours. There are ethical issues that need to be considered. Any long-distance or toll phone calls should be charged to a telephone credit card. That will also help to keep your call confidential. If you do make calls from your office, try to make them during your break times, so you are not infringing on your regular work hours with non–work-related phone calls. You will have to fit most of your letter writing, planning, and research into personal time. You may not be able to schedule as many interviews, relying instead on the telephone for most of your contacts. You may need to take time off for interviews; however, you may be able to schedule interviews for late in the day after your regular work hours or on Saturdays. It doesn't hurt to ask for this consideration.

OPTIMIZE YOUR PLAN

Now that you have a plan in mind, how do you make the best use of the three top techniques for finding jobs? Your first step was to understand yourself by defining your Ideal Position (Section One) and by researching and obtaining information about your job prospects (Section Two).

RESEARCH YOUR PROSPECTS

Your job search will be most effective if you maintain a clear idea of your job objective and employer preferences. Conduct library research to determine who the employers are in the area of your geographical choice. Narrow down your list to include only those employers whose industry, product or service, and organizational culture are in line with your preferences.

Use business directories like *Million Dollar Directory*, published by Dun & Bradstreet, or *Standard & Poor's Register* to give you basic information about larger corporations. Specialized directories, newspaper articles, and the Yellow Pages of the telephone book can provide information about other employers. Call employers directly and ask for annual reports or company brochures. Review daily, weekly, monthly, and business newspapers and journals for help-wanted advertisements. Even if the job is not quite right for you, note which employers seem to be hiring.

Now put your knowledge into action!

Networking and Prospecting

Begin networking by asking friends and associates for information on these and other employers. Describe your Ideal Position and ask for suggestions of knowledgeable people who might be able to give you information or ideas that will help you. Remember that up to 70 percent of job openings are found through networking and prospecting, and concentrate your efforts there. Remember that networking can take place in any setting where you have an opportunity to talk with at least one other person. Don't neglect opportunities to chat with your hairdresser, dentist, attorney, minister, and other local businesspeople. They often know a tremendous number of people. Get active in local and regional business groups and professional associations and use your meetings for networking opportunities. Oftentimes, the best leads that you will receive will come from unexpected sources. People can't help you if you don't tell them what you need. Also, directly approach employers using the telephone prospecting script that you prepared earlier.

Search Firms or Employment Agencies

Determine which headhunters and agencies work with people with your background. A good source for this information is *Job Hunters Sourcebook*, published by Gale Research Inc., and the *Directory of Executive Recruiters* from Kennedy Publications. Your library should have these. Develop a "marketing letter" describing your job objective, your qualifications, your preferred industry, type of employer, and salary requirements. Always keep in mind that these firms are paid by the hiring organization, so their loyalty lies with their client, not with you. Unless they are specifically looking for someone with your background and skills, you may not hear back from them. The response rate for such letters is usually 2 percent to 3 percent, meaning that if you send out 100 such letters, you will be contacted by two or three firms. Nonetheless, if you take the time to contact these firms, you can get tapped into a job source which can be working for you without much further effort on your part. If you do get a response, try to establish a positive relationship with a single recruiter who will not only work with you on her own search, but possibly also refer you to other recruiters in her firm who may be seeking a candidate with your background and skills.

WANT ADS

Briefly review newspaper want ads daily, as well as thoroughly on Sunday, when the majority of ads run. Include area newspapers and any special business periodicals that cover your geographical choice. Locate and review want ads from trade journals and publications of professional associations that cover your field. Try to do this research late in the day or on weekends, when you can't make networking calls. Make sure your responses to the ads specifically mention the title of the want ad, the publication, and the date. Your letter should also be specific to each want ad, not a canned response you send to everyone. If you have the contact information, try following up on your letter within a few days of expected delivery in order to talk directly to the individual who will be screening the responses. This can help move you to the "yes" pile.

By allocating your job search strategies this way, you will cut down on the time it takes to be ahead of your competition and takes to find your next job.

Daily Job Search Planner

TIME	Sunday	Monday	Tuesday	Wednesday	Thursday	Friday	Saturday
7:00							
8:00							
9:00							
10:00							
11:00							
12:00							
1:00							
2:00							
3:00							
4:00							
5:00							
Evening							

Networking Contact Tracker

Name	Company	Telephone No.	Date Called	Resume Sent	Interview	Referrals	Follow-Up

Prospecting Contact Tracker

Employer	Address	Telephone No.	Contact Name	Date/Time Called	Notes

Contact Information

Name: _____

_____

Title: _____

_____

Organization: _____

_____

Address: _____

_____

Phone: _____

Fax: _____

E-mail: _____

Referred by: _____

_____

Date: _____

Notes: _____

_____

_____

_____

_____

_____

_____

_____

_____

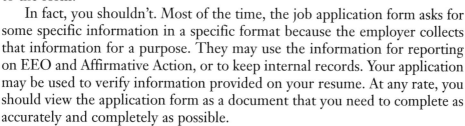

APPLICATIONS AND REFERENCES

There is a good chance that during your job search you will be asked to complete an application form. It is a good idea to have the detailed information these often require with you when you visit a company or have an interview. Also, it is quite likely that you will be asked for a list of references who are knowledgeable of your capabilities. In this chapter, the effective use of references and filling out job applications are discussed.

JOB APPLICATIONS

Completing job application forms may seem like an unimportant step in your job search. After all, you've already spent countless hours putting a lot of that information in your resume and on your reference page. Can't you just attach a copy of your resume and reference page to the form?

In fact, you shouldn't. Most of the time, the job application form asks for some specific information in a specific format because the employer collects that information for a purpose. They may use the information for reporting on EEO and Affirmative Action, or to keep internal records. Your application may be used to verify information provided on your resume. At any rate, you should view the application form as a document that you need to complete as accurately and completely as possible.

Because this is an important document in its own right, you should be careful to be neat. If necessary, ask to take the application with you to complete at home. This way, you can make a copy of it to practice on. If that is not practical, read it carefully as you complete it and make sure that you are providing the information requested in the manner requested.

Use blue or black ink and print legibly. Make sure to not leave any spaces blank. If a question does not apply to you, indicate "NA" in the space, for

"Not Applicable." The only case where you should not provide exact information is when asked for "Salary Desired." The answer to that question should be the salary range stated for the position if you know it, or simply "Negotiable" or "Will Discuss."

Some application forms ask for salary history on previous positions. This information is likely to be used to determine whether you are priced correctly for the position for which you are being considered. When questioned, about 50 percent of hiring managers admit that if the information is not provided, but the candidate still has the basic skills and experience sought, omitting the salary information will not eliminate the candidate from consideration. On the basis of this finding, you may opt to omit this information, if you fear that it will harm you in consideration for the position. Just realize that you have a 50:50 chance of being dropped from consideration by not supplying the information. If you can supply the information and develop a strategy for discussing a widely differing salary expectation, you may be better off.

In order to be able to complete application forms completely on site, you should carry with you not only your resume and reference page, but a complete work history that includes addresses and phone numbers, names and titles of former supervisors, and other detailed information not usually included on your resume. Never, never, never write "see resume" on the application form; instead, complete the requested information as asked. Do not run the risk of having your application discarded because it has not been filled out completely.

On the next page, there is a sample application form for you to practice on. You can use this as a guide for future applications that you may need to complete.

Application for Employment

PERSONAL INFORMATION

Name: _____ Date: _____

Social Security number: _____

Home address: _____

City, State, Zip: _____

Home phone: _____ Business phone: _____

US Citizen? _____ If not, give Visa number & expiration: _____

POSITION APPLYING FOR

Title: _____ Salary desired: _____

Referred by: _____ Date available: _____

EDUCATION

High school (Name, City, State): _____

Graduation date: _____

Business or technical school: _____

Dates attended: _____ Degree, major: _____

Undergraduate college: _____

Dates attended: _____ Degree, major: _____

Graduate school: _____

Dates attended: _____ Degree, major: _____

REFERENCES

_____

_____

_____

_____

_____

_____

(continued)

Application, continued.

EMPLOYMENT HISTORY

Employer: ——————————— Address: ———————————

Phone: ——————————— Starting pay: ——— Ending pay: ———

Employment dates: ——————— Job title: ———————————

Primary duties & responsibilities: ———————————

————————————————————————

Reason for leaving: ———————————————

Employer: ——————————— Address: ———————————

Phone: ——————————— Starting pay: ——— Ending pay: ———

Employment dates: ——————— Job title: ———————————

Primary duties & responsibilities: ———————————

————————————————————————

Reason for leaving: ———————————————

Employer: ——————————— Address: ———————————

Phone: ——————————— Starting pay: ——— Ending pay: ———

Employment dates: ——————— Job title: ———————————

Primary duties & responsibilities: ———————————

————————————————————————

Reason for leaving: ———————————————

Employer: ——————————— Address: ———————————

Phone: ——————————— Starting pay: ——— Ending pay: ———

Employment dates: ——————— Job title: ———————————

Primary duties & responsibilities: ———————————

————————————————————————

Reason for leaving: ———————————————

EFFECTIVE USE OF REFERENCES

At some point in your job search, you will probably be asked to present a list of personal and business references. These people will probably be contacted by mail or phone to give some feedback on you, the job candidate. Oftentimes, the information provided by these associates will be the deciding factor in the decision to offer you the position. A negative comment from one of your references can eliminate you even if you are a well-qualified candidate. Obviously, the choice of your references and their preparation for a call is extremely important.

Who should be on your reference list? The people you select as references should know you and your skills. For business references, you want to pick people who have worked with you and have a high regard for your work. Former supervisors, peers, and subordinates are good choices if you had good relationships with them. If you had a long-standing conflict with a former co-worker, don't offer that name as a reference. If it was a former supervisor, you may still be asked for the name, but you don't have to suggest it. If you must use someone with whom you had difficulty working, be candid about the situation. Explain that you had a conflict, and thus may not be given a glowing review, but that you were still able to work constructively with this individual.

Other choices might include people outside your place of employment such as salespeople, industry colleagues, or service vendors with whom you interacted on a frequent basis on company business. You can also list people with whom you worked on volunteer or civic projects. A student could consider listing a teacher or professor who has overseen a project or paper.

Personal references should preferably be people who have known you for at least a few years. These can be friends, neighbors, or co-volunteers on a project or committee. It is best not to choose relatives because their opinions won't be weighted as heavily by the employer.

Always contact the individuals that you want to list to get their approval and to prepare them. Verify the correctness of names, employers, addresses and phone numbers. Tell each person about your job search, what kinds of positions you are seeking, and how they can be of help to you in providing reference information. Stress the importance of this role and offer to fill them in on the details of your recent past, if necessary. The more information you can provide to your references, the more specific they can be in providing information about you.

Don't assume that your references know everything about you or your professional experience. Provide each reference with a copy of your resume and go through it with him or her in person stressing your experience, skills, and accomplishments. You can also outline points or qualities that you would like your references to address with a potential employer. If there are questions that you would like answered in a specific manner, let your references know.

When you list your references, include name, title, employer/organization name, address, and phone. Some of your references may request that they be contacted at home rather than at work. In that case, still include the title and employer, but indicate that a home address and phone are listed. The title and employer name help put the reference into a context. It's a good idea to type a formal reference page, with your name and address as the heading that you can give to a prospective employer at the appropriate time. See the example that follows.

The best time to provide references is at, or following, an interview. Before that time, usually the employer is not interested in having that information. Occasionally, though, you may be asked to provide letters of reference at the time you apply for a job. In that case, you will want to ask selected individuals to write directly to the organization to which you are applying. Their letters should speak directly about the job for which you want to be considered. Your references should try to be as specific as possible in discussing your experience and abilities in terms of the requirements for the particular job. In that case, your letters of reference will be used as part of the initial screening process for the job. They can be critical in determining whether you are screened in or out.

Upon leaving a job, you may have asked for or been given a letter of reference from past supervisors or co-workers. Be sure to keep the original and make extra copies to give away. These letters should be on letterhead and look as official as possible. You can provide copies of these letters along with your list of references when asked for them. Although these reference letters may look impressive, they are not used much in business today. They are still common in the academic world. However, in business, the method of choice seems to be telephone contact, which tends to be more revealing into the true nature of your character, abilities, and background. It is also interactive.

Your references are a critical part of your job search process. They should be treated with respect and care. Give your reference list only when asked to do so. Never list references on your resume. Let your references know when you have given their name to a potential employer, and provide a description of the job and company with which you have interviewed. Ask your references to let you know when they have been contacted by an employer. Usually the fact that your references have been called means that you are a serious candidate for the position.

Let your references know how much you appreciate their assistance. Thank them in writing once you have landed a new position. This will also let them know where you are working so you can stay in touch. A small gift may also be appropriate if a reference was exceptionally helpful in your job search.

Sample Reference Page

PATRICIA DIMWORTH
4 Heath Lane
Memphis, TN 37866
(615) 538-1634

REFERENCES

Business References

Robert Penworthy
Director of Sales and Marketing
Memphis Carpetland
1324 Dixie Rd.
Memphis, TN 37864
(615) 867-1923

Sally Raphael
Manager of Sales
Autoworld Tennessee
945 Rebel Highway
Memphis, TN 37836
(615) 395-3957

Joseph Campbell
Owner
Magic Copiers
396 Main Street
Memphis, TN 37926
(615) 402-4583

Personal References

Mary Worth
Chairperson
Happy Valley PTA
1459 Spring Hill Drive
Memphis, TN 37295
(615) 538-9236

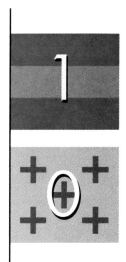

ALL ABOUT INTERVIEWS

The interview is the culmination of all of your job search preparation and research. You have already begun the preparation process by completing the exercises, identifying your Ideal Position, and researching and contacting organizations of interest to you. The final interview preparation steps involve getting ready for the interview, learning about the types of interviews, practicing interview questions, preparing questions to ask the interviewer, and interview follow-up.

GETTING READY FOR THE INTERVIEW

In anticipation for the interview, gather the following:

- Copies of your resume
- A reference list
- Important dates (employment, school, etc.)
- A folder with a pad of paper and pen to take notes
- Appropriate business clothes. Dress conservatively in a suit or dress. The first impression you make is usually a lasting one.
- Directions to the organization with information on parking and passes. (It may take several minutes to sign in at the lobby, so allow enough time.)

TYPES OF INTERVIEWS

If you have not been in the job market in recent years, you may be surprised at some of the changes that have been occurring in the staffing process. Most job seekers are accustomed to a one-on-one interview with a representative from human resources or with the hiring manager for a specific position. Usually, these interviews were done in an information gathering and evaluating format. While that is still common, you are likely to encounter one or more of the following variations, too.

Group or Team Interviews

Instead of meeting with one person, you may encounter an interview procedure that involves talking to several department members for several hours or meeting with different teams of people. Attempt to determine ahead of time who will be talking with you, their titles, and their responsibilities. Write down their names in your notebook or folder that you will be taking with you, and review the names before your interview. Knowing their titles and responsibilities will aid in anticipating their expectations and concerns. You may also ask how long you should allow for the interview so that you avoid any conflicts with other appointments. You certainly do not want to plan an hour for an interview and find the interview team expects you to stay several hours.

While it may be somewhat exhausting to interview sequentially with a number of people, it will give you a good sense of the makeup of the group with whom you may be working. You will also have a better chance to ask them individual questions about their area of responsibility. Overall, you should come away with a fairly complete picture of the organization and your possible future peers and supervisors. As you leave each person, ask for a business card, as a reminder to you and to provide the contact information you will need for a thank you letter, and possible future follow-up.

A group interview will allow you to observe the dynamics between the individuals participating in the interview, but it can be a challenge to provide attention to each person. You will have to divide your attention among the group members as they ask questions. The best approach is to keep focused on whoever is currently asking the question as it is being formulated, then try to make eye contact around the group, while directing most of it to the questioner of the moment. Try not to exclude anyone with your body language. If you have a chance to ask questions, try to cover several people's areas of responsibility to avoid focusing in on one person, and to get as much information as you can. Stay calm, and don't be afraid to adjust your seating position in order to see everyone in the group.

Telephone Interviews

In order to save time and expense, many firms now hold interviews by telephone with their initial pool of candidates in order to narrow the field down to two to five finalists. In some cases, you will be called and asked to interview on the spot; other times, you will receive a preliminary call to set a time for the actual interview. Obviously, it is to your advantage to know when the interview will occur. You can gather information, set up a quiet area, and go over your research material prior to the call. Therefore, if you are called for an on-the-spot interview and you are not ready, go ahead and say, "This is not a convenient time," or, "I was just on my way out the door for an appointment;

could we schedule a time later today or tomorrow for this call?" This is certainly a reasonable request, and you will not be hurt by asking for the delay. Find out if you will be talking with one individual, several in sequence, or to a group on a conference call. Get the names, titles, and a bit of information about whoever will be interviewing you, so you can anticipate their expectations and concerns.

To prepare for the call, make sure you have a quiet space set aside where family members and pets won't bother you. Gather any letters, notes, or information that you have pertaining to this job opportunity, and go over them to refresh your memory of the details. Go over your resume again. Also, you may want to have a glass of water, cough drops, tissues, or any other supplies that make you feel secure that you can get through the conversation uninterrupted. These calls can easily last for over an hour. Make sure that you warn your family that this is an important call and you are not to be interrupted unless it is an emergency. Then get to your area a few minutes early, take a deep breath, and smoothly sail through it. You will find that it is no worse than a face-to-face interview, and you at least can have helpful notes to look at for those tough questions.

Behavioral Interviews

A behavioral interview is an interview process where you are asked to describe situations that you have faced before and explain how you successfully handled them. They may be held in an individual or group setting. You won't know that it is a behavioral interview until the interviewer begins asking you questions. Your clue will be that most of the questions will be in a form to encourage you to share actual stories of your past work. For example:

> "Describe a time when you had to handle a difficult discussion with an employee."

> "Give me an example of how you were able to improve productivity in your department."

> "Have you ever faced a deadline you could not meet? Tell me about it."

Your task is to describe the situation and the consequences. Choose stories with a positive outcome, if possible, and give a fairly detailed recounting focusing on your decisions, actions, and the results. Your goal is to create a mental image of yourself performing the job and fitting into the organization. In fact, this technique of answering questions with a story works well in any interview setting. It is a positive way to lend credence to your answers. The theory behind behavioral interviewing is that your past behavior in a situation is a good predictor of your future behavior. The situations chosen for the interview have been selected because they represent typical situations that you might encounter on the job. Your response will demonstrate whether you share the same approach, values, knowledge, and techniques as others in the organization.

Even in a traditional information-gathering interview, answering a question with concrete examples from your past is an excellent way to illustrate to the interviewer how you would fit into the organization. Descriptive answers actually help the interviewer picture you in the job setting.

PREPARING FOR QUESTIONS

There are some general guidelines you can follow in preparing to answer typical interview questions. These guidelines will help you handle any negative events in your past, as well as help you present yourself as positively as possible, while being true to yourself. Some questions asked during interviews tend to be difficult for job seekers. Tips on answering these questions are given below.

Tell me about yourself.

Give a brief overview of your education, work history, and your current and future goals.

Practice this until you can give this "speech" in about two minutes or less.

Why do you want to work here?

Talk about the elements of the job or organization that interest you and how your Ideal Position fits this organization.

What are your greatest strengths?

Pick two or three strengths that are pertinent to this job and give examples.

What are your greatest weaknesses?

Pick one weakness and describe how you have learned to deal with it or how it can sometimes be a strength.

Why are you leaving your current job?

Give a valid reason; for example, you have been laid off, you have found that you are not challenged enough, or the job no longer fits your needs or goals. Do not speak badly of your current employer.

What kind of supervisor do you prefer?

Describe what is important to you in a boss in general management terms and give an example. Again, do not say anything negative about a previous boss.

Do you prefer to work alone or as part of a team?

In most jobs, you will need to be able to do both. If you know that the organization is oriented one way or the other, and you have the same preference, then stress the preferred style.

Give an example of a problem you have faced and how you overcame it.

When giving an example, try to paint as complete a picture as you can. Give an overall description of the problem, then describe your role in solving it. Be sure to describe what the result or benefit was in solving the problem.

What kind of salary are you looking for?

It has been said by negotiators that "he (or she) that mentions money first, loses." If possible, do not put yourself into a weak negotiating position by giving a figure. Instead, indicate your willingness to defer discussion of money until you have a clearer understanding of the job and its requirements. If pushed, ask the employer to tell you the salary range, then respond with a figure within the upper half of the range. If the interviewer will not reveal that information, and you must respond, try to give a range that would be acceptable to you and that you think covers their likely offer.

Have you ever been fired from a job?

Be honest, but also be as positive as you can. Stress your attempts to correct any problems as well as anything you have learned from the experience.

What motivates you to do a good job?

Rarely is "money" the best answer, although for some commission sales positions, it might be. Instead, think of other work values that are important to you; for example, challenge, solving problems, making a contribution, or working with others to achieve mutual goals.

Remember, it is most effective to answer questions with real-life stories. Try to be thorough with your answers, but do not ramble. Above all, listen carefully to each question and make sure you are answering what was asked.

ARTICULATING YOUR ACCOMPLISHMENTS

One question that needs special attention is, "Tell me about your accomplishments." Remember the exercises you did earlier in preparation for your resume development? While reviewing your past work history, you analyzed and described your accomplishments for each job. During your interview, you must be able to articulate these accomplishments in a coherent, verbal presentation. As part of your preparation for the interview, review your resume, focusing on the accomplishments listed. During the interview, you will present your accomplishments first by setting the stage: presenting the background for the accomplishment statement.

To do this, first describe the problem or situation that you faced. Did something require attention? Was some procedure costing too much? What was the negative impact on the organization?

Next, describe your process for solving the problem. Who was involved? How long did it take? How much did it cost?

Finally, describe the result. What benefits resulted? How did your solution add value to the organization?

EXAMPLES OF AREAS OF ACCOMPLISHMENT

The following are all possible areas of accomplishment that you might want to highlight.

- Managed a special project
- Commended by management
- Installed a new system
- Instituted a new procedure
- Saved the organization money
- Reduced absenteeism
- Increased efficiency

- Improved customer or client relations
- Met deadlines consistently
- Stayed within budget
- Learned new skills
- Led a team
- Organized a function or club
- Maintained a high grade point average while working part-time

The above is not a comprehensive list. Anything you did well, a situation that you improved, or a problem that you solved could be used. Go back to Section I and review the accomplishments you analyzed during your self-assessment.

DO'S AND DON'TS

Remember these do's and don'ts when preparing your accomplishment descriptions:

DO:

- Write out a summary of several of your major accomplishments.
- Read it over and practice delivering it.
- Tape record it and listen to it.
- Ask a friend to listen to your description and ask questions.

DON'T:

- Don't make your description too long for the time allowed in an interview.
- Don't ramble. Keep your presentation focused on the subject at hand.

OTHER GENERAL QUESTIONS YOU MAY BE ASKED

Why did you choose your current career?

How would you describe yourself?

What motivates you to put forth your greatest effort?

How has your education prepared you for your career?

Why should I hire you?

What is your definition of success?

Do you have plans for continued study?

Tell me about your hobbies.

Would you consider relocation?

Tell me about your problem-solving ability.

Tell me one thing about your last job that you disliked.

What do you like most about your job?

Tell me how you make important decisions.

Tell me about a risk you have taken and the result.

What would your former co-workers say about you?

Describe a success that makes you proud.

What do you feel it takes for a person to be successful in your field?

What is your single most noteworthy accomplishment in your present job?

Describe some noteworthy ideas that you contributed on your last (or current) position.

How did you get along with your last supervisor?

When you are under pressure, how do you react? How do you get the people around you to help?

These are practice interview questions. The most important thing that you can do before you go on an interview is to determine your communication strategy. Decide beforehand what information you want to communicate, then take responsibility for making sure you communicate it.

INTERVIEWING IS A TWO-WAY STREET

Usually, near the close of the interview, you will be given an opportunity to ask questions. This is your chance to fill in your gaps of information about the job, the employer, and your work group or boss. You can also use this as an opportunity to display some of the information you obtained during your networking and research, for example, *"I read in the* Detroit News *that your firm will be expanding in the Auto Pilot Division. How do you expect that project to affect this department?"*

Try to clarify any remaining areas of comparison before leaving the interview so that you have sufficient information to review as you decide whether to go forward with this opportunity.

Sample Questions to Ask

1. How will my performance be measured?
2. Are there opportunities for continuing education?
3. How do technological advances impact this department?
4. How does this job fit into the overall organization structure?
5. Can you describe some opportunities for further career development?
6. Is this a newly created job? If not, what happened to the last person holding this position?

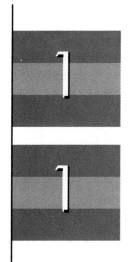

STAY THE COURSE:
THE KEY TO LANDING OPPORTUNITIES

So far in your journey to a new job, if you have planned your job search goals and executed your strategies well, you have undoubtedly begun to uncover some interesting and desirable opportunities. Now comes a key element in reaching your port—your follow-up techniques. These include thank-you notes and telephone calls. These activities accomplish a number of things:

- reinforce your memory in the mind of the decision maker
- move the decision making along
- keep you informed of the progress of the decision
- set you apart from more passive candidates

FOLLOWING UP

Thank-You Letters

After any job interview, whether a preliminary "let's get to know each other" talk or a formal first or subsequent interview, you should send a thank-you letter. It is always appropriate to prepare this type of letter in a formal business style, done on high quality paper just as you would write a cover letter. Occasionally, you may feel that a personalized, handwritten note is also appropriate, but be careful. The card you use should be a plain, conservative, good quality piece of stationery, and your handwriting should be legible. If you intend to say anything beyond a gracious "thank you," a letter is more appropriate.

In your thank-you letter, you should express appreciation for the interviewer's time and consideration. You may wish to restate your continued interest in the organization and the opportunity. You may also want to comment further on some areas of interest discussed during the interview, or add some information that you did not have a chance to share. This can be an opportunity to continue to sell yourself to the decision maker.

Close your letter by restating your understanding of the next steps in the decision-making process. If appropriate, you can indicate your intention to call and follow up. A sample letter follows on the next page.

Follow-Up Telephone Calls

Follow-up telephone calls are also an appropriate step in your job search process. If you have been told to expect a call by a certain date or within a specified time frame, make a note of it in your planner. If you do not hear from the decision maker by the agreed-upon date, place a call yourself. Be sure to be polite, and indicate that you had expected a call and are just following up on it. Sometimes, other matters interfere with the time frame for a hiring decision. You are not pushing for a decision, just making sure that the ball does not get dropped, and that you are informed along the way about the progress of the decision.

Your call may sound like this:

You: *May I speak with Mr. Sandford, please?*

Secretary: *Who's calling?*

You: *Patricia Dimworth. I'm calling to follow up on a conversation we had last week. He had indicated that he would contact me by Monday. Since it is Wednesday and I haven't heard from him, I just wanted to make sure that I hadn't missed the call.*

Secretary: *I see. Let me see if he can take your call.*

Mr. Sandford: *Ms. Dimworth, I'm glad you called. Unfortunately, we had some unexpected problems with a shipment, and I've been swamped for the last couple of days. I did want you to know that you will be invited back for a second round of interviews with my boss and the plant manager. We need to schedule those, so perhaps you could let me know what your availability is for the next two weeks.*

As you can see, you may be able to find out what caused the delay, and you may be able to go ahead and get your next round of interviews scheduled. If nothing else, your call will indicate your continued interest in the position. Since the majority of job seekers don't take this step, you will be out ahead of your competition.

NEGOTIATING THE OFFER

Many job seekers find salary negotiation to be difficult and uncomfortable. As you enter into negotiations, remember that negotiating can be defined as reaching an agreement as to what the position is worth and what your

PATRICIA DIMWORTH
4 Heath Lane
Memphis, TN 37866
(615) 538-1634
pdimworth@netgate.net

January 12, 1999

Bronze Craft of Tennessee
148 Dixie Highway
Memphis, TN 37836
Attention: Mr. Ron Sandford

Dear Mr. Sandford:

Thank you so much for the opportunity to meet with you yesterday to discuss your opening for a sales manager in your fittings division. I especially enjoyed the tour of your manufacturing facility. It certainly gave me an appreciation for the intricacies of your manufacturing and shipping processes.

As we discussed, you are looking for someone with a good working knowledge of manufacturing sales. Your products are sold both through manufacturer's representatives and through your own sales representatives. I have had experience in dealing in both situations in my most recent position, and I have a good understanding of the particular sales management concerns relevant to both. In fact, I have an excellent track record for increasing sales by using sound management and incentive programs with both types of selling. I am confident that I could produce the positive changes that you are seeking in this position.

I understand that you will be completing your first round of interviews next week. I will be looking forward to hearing from you soon after to discuss our next step.

Sincerely yours,

Patricia Dimworth

compensation should be. In a negotiation, your goal should be to get a "win-win" resolution. You and your new employer should leave the negotiation feeling that you each got a good and fair deal. This will put you on a positive footing for the start of your working relationship. The tips listed below will help lead to a successful negotiation.

1. *Know the approximate salary range for the position you are seeking.* You can obtain salary information both through your library research and through networking. Sometimes, the job description or posting states the salary range. It is important to be informed so that you position yourself correctly, neither too low nor too high. When you are informed, you are in a better position to negotiate.

2. *Determine your salary worth.* You need to know your monetary value and be able to establish your worth to the employer. Your knowledge and skill level will determine where to place yourself in your range. You may also set a "bottom-line" or "walk-away" amount. This is the amount that you have decided that you will not go below. It is similar to selling your house once you have decided that you will accept an offer of $225,000 and no less.

3. *Remember that salary is negotiable.* Usually there is some flexibility to negotiate salaries. Salaries are usually set in a range with a minimum, midrange, and maximum amount. The employer will often make an initial offer to you in the low end of the range, often expecting that you will negotiate.

4. *Realize that your starting salary is important.* The salary offer that you negotiate not only affects your present pay, but it also affects future raises that are based upon a percentage increase. Many times, your salary influences the salary of your next position as well. The amount you settle on may also create a subtle psychological impression of your value in the eyes of the employer.

5. *Let the interviewer bring up the salary issue.* "He or she who speaks first, loses" is an old cliche, but too often true. Do not bring up salary. Let the employer tell you about the compensation and benefits. Then you have the advantage of making the counteroffer.

6. *Answering the salary requirement question.* Sometimes, you will be asked to state the salary that you want during an initial interview. This is usually done with a standard question such as, "What are your salary requirements?" Your best response during the early stages of the recruiting process is to not answer with a specific salary. You may, for example, use one of these responses:

"I would have to know more specifics about the duties and responsibilities before responding."

or

"Could you tell me what the salary range is?"

or

You can also state that you would prefer to wait to talk about salary until you both have a chance to learn more about each other.

You may also be asked the salary requirement question on an application or in an initial telephone interview. You want to respond with "open" or "negotiable" until you have time to find out more about the position. Many times, this question is asked early on as a screening device to determine if your salary requirements match the salary of the position. Thus, the interviewer saves your time and his or hers by finding out if your requirements are unrealistic for the position.

7. *During the interview, remember your purpose.* Your purpose is to illustrate your worth and ability to make a contribution to the prospective organization. Once the employer is convinced that he or she wants to hire you, the balance of power in the negotiation shifts to your side.

8. *Discuss salary when the timing is right.* We have all heard the expression, "Timing is everything." Well, it is true in salary negotiations as well. Be sure not to discuss salary until the end of the interviewing process when the employer is convinced of your value.

When the salary question comes up, your first step is to summarize the job responsibilities and duties as you understand them. For example, "As I understand it, I would report directly to the president and would be responsible for setting and implementing design policy. I would have a staff of 10 who have 200 employees reporting to them. Are there any other responsibilities that I should know about?"

When you are asked your salary requirements, first find out what the salary range is for the position. You might say, "What is the normal range in your company for a position such as this?" Usually the interviewer will share with you the requested salary range. You may want to ask one more question: "For someone with my background and expertise, what would be the expected salary range?"

When you receive an offer, you have four basic choices:

1. Accept as is.
2. Negotiate for more money on the spot.
3. Delay by asking for time to consider.
4. Tell the employer that the figure is unacceptable and end the negotiations.

Don't be afraid to ask for time to consider the offer, but be reasonable. If the position is open or soon will be, the employer is likely to want to fill it as soon as possible, assuming you are considered a good candidate. Be sure the time you need to consider the offer is acceptable to the employer. Usually 24 to 48 hours is not a problem.

Use the time to consider your options. Review your Ideal Position. Does this position measure up? Look at your life management issues and ask yourself how this job will affect your personal life. Does this job mesh with your mission statement? Look at the complete salary and benefit package. You may find that there are elements of the benefit package that offset a slightly lower salary figure. Look also for items in the offer that you might bring into the negotiation to use as trade-offs.

If you elect to negotiate for more money, you may want to say something like this:

"I am pleased to have received an offer from you."

or:

"I am very impressed with your organization and the possibilities that this job offers; however, I think that the responsibilities of the position would make $$$ to $$$ more realistic for me."

Chances are good that the employer is working within a salary range that overlaps your request. After you have presented your counteroffer, be quiet, and let the employer come back with an answer. Be prepared to back up your request with evidence and justification. Remember to affirm your interest and high regard for the opportunity and keep in mind that this should be a "win-win" situation. Both you and the employer should end up feeling that you have made a good deal. If you have special needs or desires, you can often get agreement on them. For example, you may be covered under your spouse's benefit plan for medical coverage. Sometimes you can decline coverage and get the cost rolled into salary. You may be able to begin earning vacation time faster or get leave time for an already scheduled vacation. This is the time to ask any questions that you would like answered.

If you receive an offer and you have been talking to other companies as well, by all means let them know that you have received an offer. This gives them the opportunity to escalate their hiring processes and make offers of their own.

If you are intimidated by the thought of negotiating, you probably won't do well at it unless you practice beforehand. However, if there are some major parts of the offer that you strongly feel need to be adjusted to fit your needs, it may be better for you to try to negotiate rather than to accept something that will leave you feeling dissatisfied. That is not the best way to begin a new job. If you handle this in an objective and reasonable manner, you and your employer may come to a mutually beneficial arrangement.

Ten Tips to Getting a Stalled Job Search Back on Track

Many job seekers start their job search journey with great enthusiasm. First, you carefully prepare a resume taking into account your skills, accomplishments, experience, and education. You then engage in a great deal of job search activities such as making networking and prospecting contacts, as well as responding to want ads. But if you do not land a job within a couple of months, suddenly you run out of ideas for new leads and your job search stalls. At this time, you may have a sense of desperation and feeling of hopelessness. You feel that everything that can be done has been done. You're sure there are no openings at this time, so now what? At this point, many times job seekers will relax their efforts—thinking that they have done all there is to do—and wait for an opportunity to present itself. These assumptions, beliefs, and inactivity can quickly lead to a derailed job search. Here are some tips to help you reevaluate and reconstruct a new plan to get your stalled job search back on track.

1. Make and keep your job search your #1 priority.

Continue to treat your job search as a full-time activity. Do not ease up on your job search activities. Make sure that all other activities occur outside of "working hours." It is very tempting to take care of a few things around the house while you have the time. Be very deliberate about scheduling and protecting your job search time. Let family and friends know your schedule and expectations. It is easy for them to think, "Robert's home, maybe he could baby-sit or help out with some family commitments." Renew your commitment to your search and treat it as your most important endeavor. After all, your job search activities are an investment in your future and should be taken very seriously by you and your family.

2. Assess and diagnose your job search activities.

Review your job search activities to date including your daily, weekly, and monthly activities and accomplishments. Look at your number of networking contacts, prospecting contacts, association meetings, interviews, and appointments. Look for trends. Be objective. Has your activity level decreased over time? Have you contacted only people with whom you feel comfortable and avoided other contacts? Are you doing enough for your job search? Are you focused with clear objectives in mind? Is your resume working for you, or does it need to be revised to fit your current goals? This information provides a baseline from which you can set goals and plan your future activities.

3. Develop a fresh game plan and set goals.

After assessing your activities, look at your search from a fresh perspective and establish a new set of priorities and goals. Set goals that are specific, measurable, and attainable. Your new goals may include such activities as revisiting network and prospecting contacts as well as deleting ones that look like they will result in a dead end.

4. Establish a routine and keep active on a regular basis.

Establish a routine. For example, every Monday, go to the library. On Tuesday and Thursday mornings, make your contact calls to set up appointments. Follow up with your correspondence every afternoon. Organize your schedule and pace yourself so that you have a regular routine that works well for you.

Increase your level of activity. Your level of activity strongly influences the success of your job search. Increase your number of networking and prospecting contacts. For example, set a goal of increasing your contacts by 20 percent, or if your numbers are low, double the number of contacts.

Keep active on a regular basis. Don't start, pause, start, stop. Instead, keep up regular, consistent, disciplined activity.

5. Reassess your job prospects.

Review your files of targeted companies. Which ones are still of interest to you? Which ones have experienced changes in personnel or new developments? Do you need to add more organizations to your targeted list? Do you need to revisit any of the contacts you have made or contact anyone else in the organization?

6. Research, research, research.

The research process is ongoing. Schedule regular trips to the library and continue to research companies and organizations that match your job target. Include industry trade publications and newspapers as well as directories and database searches as you look for information and new developments. Read articles about people in your industry. Contact the ones who are relevant to your search.

7. Network with a purpose in mind.

Review your networking list. Who has your resume? What suggestions have they made? Have you followed up on the salient suggestions? Have you been back in touch with your networking contacts? You may want to schedule another appointment with each of your networking contacts.

Be sure to network with a purpose in mind. Are you looking for advice, a referral, or information? Your networking contacts may have new ideas for you. They are constantly meeting new people and getting new information. They may have ideas and suggestions today that they did not have a few months ago.

8. Stay active.

Stay personally, physically, and professionally active. Don't lose your drive. Make sure you schedule these activities, including exercise. Family, friends, and professional endeavors are critical to your mental and physical health.

9. Keep up on industry, community, and civic involvement.

Review the calendar of industry events. Review membership lists for networking and prospecting ideas. Make appointments with fellow professionals for before, after, and during professional meetings. Call and arrange to sit with a contact at the meeting or have a cup of coffee prior to the meeting. Continue your involvement in community and civic activities.

10. Recycle your contacts.

If your job search has gone on for a few months, chances are your contacts are cold and stale. Refresh your contacts. Get in touch again. Things change.

Where there was not an opening two months ago, there may be an opening developing today. Let your contacts know that you are still in the market.

Many job seekers make the mistake of talking to a contact only once and thinking it is enough. Until you are employed, it is *not* enough. Keep meticulous records of every contact you make, including the date and the essence of the conversation. Refer back to your notes.

Remember, the contacts made and the knowledge and information acquired during a job search are the foundation for your future. Conducting a methodical and directed search is an investment in your professional future, so get your boat off the rocks and go on to smooth sailing.

Embarking on Your New Journey

Once you've landed your new job, you want to be sure to start out on the right foot with your new boss and co-workers. Whether you have been hired to keep things running smoothly, or have been hired to "shake things up," you may need the support and assistance of existing staff. One of your first goals should be to learn as much as possible about your new organization and the people who work there. Listening and asking questions can provide you with a solid background information and understanding that can be invaluable to you as you learn your new job. Be prepared to share information about yourself, too; your new co-workers will be curious about you. Just be careful about how you present yourself; some curiosity is generated by fear, and your co-workers may be looking for reassurance that your presence is not going to jeopardize their jobs. Once you have gained an understanding of the people around you and their roles and methods of working, you will be better able to plan for changes that you need to make to do your job better.

As you progress in your new job, take time to collect important data, documents, and information that will help you make future decisions about your career. A portfolio like this might include congratulatory memos, copies of performance reviews, thank-you letters, completed reports or publications, newsletter articles about you or projects you have worked on, and other information that will help you remember your accomplishments. You can use such a portfolio as documentation to improve your rating during a performance review, and, of course, for revising your resume in the future.

You should revise your resume regularly, at least every one to two years, even if you have no intention of leaving your employer. You need to be reminded of what is important to you, not only for your own sense of understanding where you are in your life's goals, but also to help you talk about yourself with your boss for your future development.

Your career is constantly moving. You want to be able to manage it as much as possible, and to do that, you have to know where you want to go and where you have been.

Good luck. Sail away . . . and Bon Voyage!

INDEX